Mexico City through History and Culture

British Academy Occasional Paper · 13

Mexico City through History and Culture

Edited by
Linda A. Newson & John P. King

Published for THE BRITISH ACADEMY
by OXFORD UNIVERSITY PRESS

Oxford University Press, Great Clarendon Street, Oxford OX2 6DP

Oxford New York

Auckland Cape Town Dar es Salaam Hong Kong Karachi
Kuala Lumpur Madrid Melbourne Mexico City Nairobi
New Delhi Shanghai Taipei Toronto

With offices in
Argentina Austria Brazil Chile Czech Republic France Greece
Guatemala Hungary Italy Japan Poland Singapore
South Korea Switzerland Thailand Turkey Ukraine Vietnam

Published in the United States
by Oxford University Press Inc., New York

First published 2009

British Library Cataloguing in Publication Data
Data available

Library of Congress Cataloging in Publication Data
Data available

Typeset by
J&L Composition Ltd, Filey, North Yorkshire
Printed in Great Britain
on acid-free paper by
CPI Antony Rowe
Chippenham, Wiltshire

ISBN 978-0-19-726446-1

Foreword

On 30 October 2007, the symposium *Celebrating the City: Mexico City through History and Culture* took place at the British Academy in London. This event was of great importance for two main reasons, because of the prestige of the Academy in the cultural world of the United Kingdom, and because of the relevance of the subject: Mexico City, whose rich tradition represents the Old World within the New World and contributes to the city's complex and contemporary vitality.

Mexico City and London, in their contrasting traditions, share as a common feature a very deep historical *gravitas*, playing central roles in their national landscapes. These two great capitals carry the footprints of unique historical moments, and both Mexico City and London have been able to retain to our days the same cultural vitality.

This first symposium showed us the way for future scholarly exchanges, because beyond their immediate results, gatherings such as these have long-lasting effects that foster communication and challenges.

The essays here presented show through history, literature, and cinema the extraordinary richness and energy of Mexico's capital. We can say in the spirit of Julio Cortázar that they succeeded in going *around Mexico City in eighty worlds*.

Juan José Bremer de Martino
Ambassador of Mexico to the United Kingdom

Contents

List of Illustrations   ix
Notes on Contributors   xi

Introduction   I
    LINDA A. NEWSON & JOHN P. KING

I   PROLOGUE

1. *Mexico City: Space to Mourn, Time to Spend*   9
    CARLOS MONSIVÁIS

II HISTORY

2. THE PRE-COLUMBIAN CITY   21
    Tenochtitlan: the First Mexico City
    WARWICK BRAY

3. THE COLONIAL CITY   39
    Imperial Mexico: the Viceregal Capital
    D. A. BRADING

4. THE MODERN CITY   55
    From the Reforma-Peralvillo to the Torre Bicentenario:
    the Clash of 'History' and 'Progress' in the Urban Development
    of Modern Mexico City
    DIANE E. DAVIS

III CULTURE

5. THE POETIC CITY   85
    From the Consecration to the Degradation of Spring:
    the Poet in the Street
    VICENTE QUIRARTE

6.   THE CINEMATIC CITY   105
     A City Created by Film: Mexico City in Movies, 1977–2007
        HUGO LARA CHÁVEZ

7.   THE PHOTOGRAPHIC CITY   121
     A City Heading in the Opposite Direction
        MAGALI TERCERO

List of Illustrations

Figure

1.1.   Holy Saturday. Swimming pool in eastern Mexico City
       © Francisco Mata Rosas.   11

1.2.   Solidarity. Mexico City metro. © Francisco Mata Rosas.   14

1.3.   Free Time. Mexico City metro. © Francisco Mata Rosas.   16

2.1.   The Basin of Mexico in 1519. From Richard F. Townsend,
       The Aztecs (London: Thames and Hudson, 1992), p. 27.
       © Thames and Hudson.   24

2.2.   Part of an early sixteenth-century map showing the
       chinampa area. Courtesy Warwick Bray.   28

2.3.   Schematic map of Tenochtitlan-Tlatelco. From Richard F.
       Townsend, *The Aztecs* (London: Thames and Hudson,
       1992), p. 29. © Thames and Hudson.   31

2.4.   Bernardino de Sahagún's plan of the Great Precinct of
       Tenochtitlan. Courtesy Warwick Bray.   33

2.5.   View of the Zócalo with a photomontage of the
       Templo Mayor. From *Les Aztèques: Les trésors du Mexique
       ancien*, Exhibition Catalogue Musées Royaux d'Art et
       d'Histoire, Brussels 1987. © Musées Royaux d'Art et
       d'Histoire, Brussels.   35

3.1.   The 1736–1737 epidemic of 'matlazahuatl'. Cayetano de
       Cabrera y Quintero, *Escudo de armas de México* (Mexico,
       1746).   49

4.1.   Design of the proposed Torre Bicentenario, Mexico City.
       © Office for Metropolitan Architecture.   57

4.2.   Vacant workshops of Súper Servicio Lomas. Photograph
       by Gareth Jones.   59

4.3.   Conjunctures of preservation and progress, 1950–2007.   64

4.4. Tensions surrounding preservation and progress, 1950–2007. 66

4.5. Historic preservation timeline, Mexico City's Centro. 68

4.6. Suspension of building works authorized by INAH, downtown Mexico City, October 2007. Photograph by Onesimo Flores Dewey. 76

4.7. Renovation of historic commercial street, downtown Mexico City, January 2008. Photograph by Onesimo Flores Dewey. 77

5.1. Carl Nebel, *American Troops in Mexico City*, 13 September 1847. 93

5.2. Alfredo Zalce. *Mexico Becomes a Great City* (1947). From *Pasado y presente del Centro Histórico*. México City: Fomento Cultural Banamex, 1993, p. 96. 99

6.1. *Lola* (1987). Still by Guadalupe Sánchez. 107

6.2. *El callejón de los milagros* (1995). Still by Federico García. 109

6.3. *Cadena perpetua* (1978). Still by Ángel Corona. 112

6.4. *Amores perros* (2000). Still by Federico García. 115

6.5. *Sexo, pudor y lágrimas* (1998). Still by Daniel Daza. 115

6.6. *Principio y fin* (1993). Still by Federico García. 116

6.7. *Batalla en el cielo* (2005). Courtesy Fernanda Romandía. 117

7.1 Prostitute, Mexico City, 1999. © Maya Goded. 123

7.2. Morgue, Mexico City, 2003. © Maya Goded. 127

7.3. Mistreated child, Mexico City, 1997. © Maya Goded. 129

Notes on Contributors

David Brading is Emeritus Professor of Mexican History at the University of Cambridge and is a Fellow of the British Academy. He is generally recognized as the leading foreign historian on Mexico. In November 2002 he was awarded the Aztec Eagle, the highest decoration for a foreign citizen given by the Mexican government. He has published extensively on colonial Latin America, and is author of a number of widely praised volumes, including *The First America: The Spanish Monarchy, Creole Patriots, and the Liberal State, 1492–1867* (1991) and *Mexican Phoenix: Our Lady of Guadalupe: Image and Tradition across Five Centuries* (2001).

Warwick Bray is Emeritus Professor of Latin American Archaeology at the Institute of Archaeology, UCL. His publications on the Aztecs include the well-known book *Everyday Life of the Aztecs* (1968). He has excavated widely in Latin America, particularly in Colombia and Ecuador, and his specialized interests include pre-European agriculture, land use and gold working.

Diane Davis is Professor of Political Sociology and Head of the International Development Group in the Department of Urban Studies and Planning at MIT, where she was formerly Associate Dean of the School of Architecture and Planning. Her research focuses on urban political economy, leftist mayors in the developing world, and the challenge of metropolitanism in a globalizing Latin America, primarily in Mexico. In 1994 she published a major study of the impact of industrialization in Mexico City entitled *Urban Leviathan: Mexico City in the Twentieth Century*. Since then much of her work has been comparative in nature and includes *Discipline and Development: Middle Classes and Economic Prosperity in East Asia and Latin America* (2004), which was awarded Best Book in Political Sociology by the American Sociological Association (2005). She has been both a John D. and Catherine T. MacArthur Fellow (1999–2000) and Carnegie Scholar (2001–3).

John King is Professor of Latin American Cultural History and Director of the Humanities Research Centre at the University of Warwick. He has published a dozen edited and single-authored books on Latin American culture, including, most recently, *The Role of Mexico's Plural in Latin American Literary and Political Culture* (2007).

Hugo Lara is a film critic and researcher. He has worked at the Mexican Film Institute (IMCINE), at the Office of Visual Media at the National Council for Arts and Culture (CONACULTA) and has collaborated with Educational Television and TV UNAM. In 1991, he was awarded first prize in the distinguished film critic contest organized by CONACULTA and the DICINE Magazine; he has contributed to several specialized film magazines and national newspapers, including *El Universal* and *Reforma*, and he is author of *Una ciudad inventada por el cine* (2006). In February 2008, he was the curator of a photo exhibition about Mexico City and its films, in Chapultepec Park. He is currently a member of the group that is planning the National Film Museum in Mexico, to be opened in 2010.

Carlos Monsiváis is generally regarded as Mexico's leading cultural critic, and Mexico City's greatest living chronicler. He is said to have pioneered the genre of *nueva crónica*, and has written extensively about Mexican history, culture and politics. His best-known works include *Días de guardar* (1970), *Amor perdido* (1977) and *Escenas de pudor y liviandad* (1981), which won the Jorge Cuesta Literary Award. He has won Spain's Premio Anagrama de Ensayo, and the Anagrama International Literature Prize for *Aires de familia: cultura y sociedad en América Latina* (2000). Other honours include the National Journalism Award (1977), the National Literary Award (2005), and the Juan Rulfo Literary Award (2006).

Linda Newson is Professor of Geography at King's College London, where she was formerly Head of the School of Humanities. She has undertaken extensive archival research in Latin America and authored five books examining different aspects of the impact of Spanish colonial rule. Her most recent work (with Susie Minchin) is *From Capture to Sale: The Portuguese Slave Trade to Spanish South America in the Early Seventeenth Century* (2007). In 1992 she received the C.O. Sauer award for distinguished scholarship from the Conference of Latin Americanist Geographers in the USA and in 1993 the Back Award from the Royal Geographical Society for her contributions to the historical geography of Latin America. In 2000 she was elected Fellow of the British Academy, and is the current Chair of the British Academy's Latin America and the Caribbean Area Panel.

Vicente Quirarte is Professor of Literature at the Universidad Nacional Autónoma de México. He has lectured throughout Mexico and abroad, and has held the Rosario Castellanos Chair at the Hebrew University in Jerusalem. He has published poetry, narrative, theatre, literary criticism and historical essays. A collection of his poems was published under the title *Reasons of Samurai* (UNAM) (2000), and his other works include *Peces del* *aire altísimo. Poesía y poetas en México* (1993) and *Elogio de la calle: biografía literaria de la Ciudad de México* (2001).

Magali Tercero is a journalist and editor. She has recently published *Cien freeways: DF y alrededores* (2006), which was awarded the National Prize for an Urban Chronicle by UACM in 2005, and *Frida Kahlo: una mirada crítica* (2007). An essay in the latter has been included in *A ustedes les consta: antología de la crónica en México*, edited by Carlos Monsiváis, and in *Los mejores ensayos mexicanos*, by Antonio Saborit. In 2007 she received the Prize for Excellence in the category of chronicle awarded by the Interamerican Press Society (Sociedad Interamericana de Prensa) in Miami. She contributes to *Laberinto*, the cultural supplement of *Milenio Diario*, and has collaborated in the Mexican edition of *El País*. She is a member of the Sistema Nacional de Creadores de Arte (SNCA).

Introduction

LINDA A. NEWSON & JOHN P. KING

This volume arises out of a symposium entitled 'Celebrating Cities: Mexico City through History and Culture' held at the British Academy in October 2007. The symposium developed from a desire of the British Academy's Latin American and Caribbean Panel to develop collaborative research links with specific countries in the region. Mexico was a priority and so contact was made with the Mexican Embassy to the United Kingdom in London; its cultural attaché, Ignacio Durán Loera, suggested that we might hold a joint symposium on Mexico City. Together we decided that the symposium should focus on the city's history and culture and that we would invite eminent scholars from different fields to reflect on Mexico City at a particular time period or from a specific cultural perspective. The speakers were given a deliberately broad brief, because our intention was not to produce a collection of textbook-type essays, but to learn about their particular perspectives on Mexico City as eminent scholars in their fields.

As with any city of over twenty million inhabitants, it is easy to point to many problems that Mexico City faces, such as social inequality, traffic congestion and environmental degradation, which are often made worse by inadequacies in city governance and management. But these are problems that face all major world cities, such as New York, London or Beijing. Nevertheless, even those scholars who are critical of Mexico City's development retain a deep affection for the city. Attracted by its vitality, they remain optimistic about its future. Building on these sentiments the aim of the symposium was therefore to celebrate Mexico City as a centre of cultural creativity, diversity and dynamism, tracing its history from the foundation of Tenochtitlan in 1324 to the present day.

The opening address was given by Carlos Monsiváis who, for some fifty years, has been the most influential and engaging commentator on the transformations of Mexico City. He has made his own the urban *crónica*, or chronicle, which, as Vicente Quirarte points out in Chapter 5, has had a long and distinguished lineage in Mexico. The *crónica* has been usefully defined as an 'in-between' genre that falls between historical and fictional narrative. In his chapter, Carlos Monsiváis offers a series of snapshots of the 'post-apocalyptic' city. He looks at the many different ways in which ordinary people negotiate and appropriate urban space—or rather the lack of space—in Mexico City. He blends humour and political and social criticism with a great affection for the travails of working or marginal people. Monsiváis is a uniquely popular figure in Mexico. At the symposium one of the participants told an illustrative anecdote (whether it is true or apocryphal is not the point: it is part of urban legend). Some years ago, Monsiváis was sitting in a restaurant in Mexico City when an armed gang entered and demanded the wallets and jewellery of the diners (one of the 'secuestros express' or express robberies dramatized in the 1998 movie *Todo el poder*, analysed in Chapter 6). 'Not you, Mr Monsiváis' they shouted over to his table, 'you carry on eating.' In the recent novel by Roberto Bolaño, *The Savage Detectives,* which focuses on student life in Mexico in the mid-seventies, Monsiváis is a constant presence, a guide for the young 'detectives' through the topographical, cultural and political labyrinth of the city. In this paper he offers a similar guide to what he has called, as a title of a book of his essays, 'the rituals of chaos': the way in which the city functions seemingly against the odds, the enormous energy and fascination of everyday life. This chapter is illustrated with the work of Francisco Mata Rosas, himself one of Mexico City's most illuminating photographic chroniclers.

Judged by any criteria Mexico City was and is one of the world greatest cities. Few are probably aware that its predecessor, Tenochtitlan, had a population of between about 200,000 and 300,000 when the Spanish arrived in 1521. It was far larger than most European cities at the time, including London which only had about 50,000 inhabitants; today it is still about twice the size of London. Yet, like London, Mexico City has grown organically, largely developed by waves of immigrants with new ideas and aspirations. While they have often envisioned the city in new ways, whether by design or not, they have been unable to escape totally its historical past and indeed at times have positively embraced it to serve contemporary political ends. Mexico City is thus a palimpsest built up over nearly 700 years.

The popular image of the Aztecs is one of a barbaric society dedicated to the blood-thirsty sacrifice of thousands of human captives a year. However, Warwick Bray's attempt in Chapter 2 to visualize how Tenochtitlan may have looked and functioned indicates that underneath this 'exotic' surface, by any criteria used to define civilizations, such as the existence of a functioning bureaucracy, sophisticated agricultural technology, monumental architecture, and ceremonialism, it was a truly civilized city. It was developed by a society that had risen from humble beginnings, and the great capital the Aztecs created became a symbol of their power and of the culture and beliefs that had brought them success. While the city buildings were destroyed by the Spanish invaders, elements of its culture lingered on in the daily life and memories of its inhabitants.

The Spanish empire was an urban-based empire, and when the Spanish arrived in Mexico, they had a different idea of what a civilized city should be. They symbolically built their own city on the site of the destroyed Aztec capital and imposed their authority through the construction of a regular grid plan that reflected their conception of a social order. In Chapter 3 David Brading demonstrates that, while the Spanish had a clear vision of what the city should be, the city of the conquistadors was relatively short lived for it was soon transformed by its Creole inhabitants who stamped their own identity on its buildings and culture. Even as early as the seventeenth century some Creoles, let alone the native inhabitants, began looking back to the glorious past the conquistadors had destroyed. Yet the city's development was constrained by its status as the viceregal capital of New Spain, which depended on political decisions and cultural influences emanating from Spain. Out of this tension emerged a creative process of change in which different ethnic groups and cultures intermingled and conflicted to ensure that the character and social composition of Mexico City would be different from that in other cities in Spanish America. Yet the changes were not brought about without loss. Due to conquest, over-work and Old World diseases, the population of the Mexico City fell to about 50,000 in 1600, and as Brading shows, epidemics, floods and earth-quakes continued to afflict the city periodically throughout the colonial period.

The Enlightenment and Independence periods brought further changes to the physical character of Mexico City as the newly independent nation of Mexico sought to stamp an independent, secular and pro-gressive image on its capital. New monumental buildings that sometimes incorporated pre-Columbian motifs were constructed and public health measures that involved widening roads and developing drainage and sewer-age systems brought significant changes to the physical infrastructure of the city. This modernization process has continued to the present, but as Diane Davis illustrates in Chapter 4, it has not been without considerable debate and conflict. Her detailed account of struggles over the portrayal of the city's image and over the preservation of historic buildings, teases out questions of the role of different social groups (the middle classes, preserva-tionists, property developers, street vendors) and the political alliances they have forged to promote change or preserve the past. But the past is not a single entity and if preservation is to be pursued, the question arises as to what periods of history represented in the city are to be favoured in its future development. This question will be familiar to governments of historic cities, but the institutional and bureaucratic context in which decisions are made and the images that Mexico City wishes to portray perhaps make its historic past more immediate. Davis argues that at present the city is caught between the past and the future. This observation might be applied to any period in the city's history since its foundation, but over time it has acquired more and more layers and what it symbolizes to its inhabitants and how they experience the city and has become fragmented by social class and ethnicity. There is not one Mexico City but many.

This diversity is explored in three chapters that analyse different cultural representations of the city. Vicente Quirarte in Chapter 5 offers a panoramic overview of how poets and poetry have reflected and created Mexico City, from the time of Tenochtitlan to the early twenty-first century. He focuses, in particular, on the mid-nineteenth century onwards, a time when, as Walter Benjamin has demonstrated in his study of the work of Charles Baudelaire, the city became a central protagonist of lyric poetry. In an account that is rich in illustrations from the poets themselves, he shows how the writers have read the city and how the city itself has transformed their texts and their way of life. In Quirarte's terms, the poet can be many things: an urban planner, a privileged insider who can translate the city's transformations and emotions, a 'biographer of emotions', a cartographer, charting the invisible map of Mexico City. From King Nezahualcóyotl to the poet Eduardo Lizalde in the late twentieth century, poets have found ways of describing and celebrating the city without falling into despair, for according to Quirarte, the very naming and exploration of despair is a way of transcending it.

Hugo Lara in Chapter 6 argues that the development of cinema over more than a century is bound up with developments in the city. While national cinema always looked to show the sweep and scope of the entire country, it would return insistently to the capital city as its major source of inspiration, as both a setting and as a main actor. For Lara, Mexican cinema has always offered a mirror that refracts developments within the city: the cityscape, the buildings, the wide avenues and the narrow backstreets, certain privileged spaces (the neighbourhood, the tenement buildings), and the inhabitants, in particular the family. His chapter focuses in particular on the period 1977–2007, and it shows how certain defining moments—the earthquake of 1985, the dream and the realities of globalization, the defeat of the PRI in the 2000 elections—are woven into narratives and images that explore dislocation, isolation and different forms of resistance.

The power of the image is also explored in Magali Tercero's presentation (Chapter 7), which provides a series of chronicles on contemporary urban life that gloss certain images by the photographer Maya Goded. In the photos and in the chronicles, the world of the child, the prostitute and the desolation of death are explored. In the chronicles unaccompanied by photos, Tercero paints vibrant portraits of a woman's prison, the mass rallies of the Zapatistas in the main square of the city and the attractions of *lucha libre* (masked wrestling) and the national lottery. Wrestling and the lottery are both seen as ways in which the inhabitants of the city can step out of their normal everyday lives for a few minutes or hours, and inhabit another world, of desire, where they can dream alternative realities. The historians, the chroniclers, the poets, the filmmakers, the cinematographers, the photographers have all captured or created, in their different genres and styles, aspects of the city. We hope that this volume offers another small window onto this dynamic, constantly evolving space that is Mexico City.

The editors would like to thank the Mexican Embassy and the British Academy for their generous support for the symposium and for the publication of this volume. We would particularly like to thank the Mexican Cultural Attaché to the UK, Ignacio Durán Loera, for his enthusiasm and support throughout the project, and in particular for his help in recruiting such eminent Mexican scholars. We would also like to thank all the contributors for their wholehearted support for the symposium and this publication and for responding so quickly to editorial questions. We have indeed been privileged to work with such excellent scholars and colleagues. Finally, thanks are due to Jimena Gorráez Belmar at the Mexican Embassy and Rachel Paniagua at the British Academy without whose efforts and collaboration neither the symposium nor this publication would have materialized.

I
PROLOGUE

1.

Mexico City: Space to Mourn, Time to Spend

CARLOS MONSIVÁIS

For John King

Visually, Mexico City signifies above all else the superabundance of people who—for strange reasons from my point of view—need more people. Loneliness is the cruellest word, mixing memory and secret hopes, and intimacy is by permission only, the 'poetic licence' that allows you, momentarily, to forget the worse curse of them all: you, inhabitant of Mexico City, forget the dogma: here you'll never die alone, even if you suffered a heart attack in a lonely elevator.[1] No use. At the moment of your last sigh, someone will ask you: 'Excuse me, pal, do you need a priest, a doctor or a camera crew?' *Lasciati ogni speranza*, Robinson Crusoe.

Turmoil is the repose of the city dweller, a whirlwind set in motion by secret harmonies and lack of public resources. How can one describe Mexico City today? Like every megalopolis, you see mass overcrowding and a new set of emotions, sensations, sensibilities; the ever shrinking space, where many traditions are newly born, and because everything works thanks only to what we call 'a miracle'—which is no more than the meeting place of the basic decency of the majority, hard work (every family is the cathedral of sense), good luck, technology, solidarity and the frustration of logical thinking. I will now enumerate some of the most frequent or unusual images of the capital city:

—multitudes on the metro, where almost five or six million travellers a day are crammed, making space for the very idea of space (blessed are the bodies that levitate);

---

[1] This chapter draws on translations of my work contained in the following: *Mexican Postcards*, trans. and ed. John Kraniauskas (London: Verso, 1997); Michael J. Dear, Gustavo Leclerc and Jo-Anne Berelowitz, eds, *Postborder City: Cultural Spaces of Bajalta California* (London: Routledge, 2003); and Rubén Gallo, ed., *The Mexico City Reader*, trans. Lorna Scott Fox (Madison: University of Wisconsin Press, 2004).

—twenty thousand naked bodies in the Zócalo or Plaza Mayor waiting for the orders of the artist-photographer Spencer Tunick (and I'll show you fear for the garment industry);

—multitudes taking their entrance exam in the (big) University Stadium;

—masked wrestlers, the tutelary gods of the new Teotihuacan of the ring ('Oh, please, dear Felipe de Jesús, our first saint, let me give you some advice: wear a mask and your flock will never end');

—the underground economy that overflows onto the pavements, making popular market places of the streets and, at certain times of day, of the slow highways (With God and Scarlet as my witnesses, I swear I saw a priest administering the last rites in a traffic jam). At traffic lights young men and women attempt to sell Kleenex, bestsellers, kitchenware, toys, tricks, fake i-Pods, pirate DVDs. The young boy, a fire-swallowing artist, blows the flame at us. On the metro five or six fakirs, with a bed of nails, argue with passengers ('This is for real. Try it/ No, you're like politicians, full of lies'). Anyway, for the time being, streets vendors are away from the Centro Histórico, hopefully for good;

—mansions built like ancient fortresses (the kitsch of bourgeois security), with private armies who may one of these days declare war on private security forces in Iraq;

—diminishing water supply, to the point that now some people recommend you guard water in safes, like jewels;

—people who, regardless of social class and very different upbringing, speak the same language (in Spanish), giving the city the aspect of a mono-lingual Tower of Babel. The same shared vocabulary, the same four-letter or eight-letter words (the most popular being *chingada*), different accents;

—the everlasting symbols: the Centro Histórico, and in the Zócalo: the Palacio Nacional: Power, History, Fate; the Cathedral: belief in a land of religious illiteracy as the bishops say; the Templo Mayor: Indian grandeur; the Zócalo itself, where every conceivable thing happens in homage to every inconceivable thing that also happens here; some agonizing rituals like the burning of Judas, big cardboard figures representing each year's villains, for instance, George Bush, Dart Vader, ex-President Vicente Fox; the Basilica of Guadalupe, the centre of faith and, in the surroundings, the Cathedral of beatific Kitsch;

—the swarm of cars. Suddenly it feels as if all the cars on Earth were held up right here, the traffic jam having now become second nature to a species hoping to arrive late for the Last Judgement. 'Forgive me, oh Lord, my soul got trapped in a jam.' Between four and six o'clock in the morning there is some relief, the species seems drowsy . . . but suddenly everything moves on again, the advance cannot be stopped. And then, the car becomes a

Figure 1.1   Holy Saturday. Swimming pool in eastern Mexico City. © Francisco Mata Rosas.

prison on wheels, the cubicle where you can hear the classics in the University of Noble Despair.

The images are few. One could add the Museum of Anthropology, the Ciudad Universitaria, and the sanctuaries of wealth: San Ángel, el Pedregal, Santa Fe, Lomas Altas, Bosques de las Lomas, Tepito (that's a private joke). The typical repertoire is now at your disposal, and if I do not include the *mariachis* of Plaza Garibaldi, it is because this text does not come with musical accompaniment. Mexico: another great Latin American city, with its seemingly uncontrollable growth, its irresponsible love of modernity made visible in skyscrapers, malls, fashion shows, spectacles, exclusive restaurants, motorways, cell phones. It's the reign of the God Internet and the Goddess Civilization, and of course a billion prayers: 'Pain, pain, go to Spain and never come back again.' Chaos, the order of the new millennium, displays its aesthetic offerings, and next to the pyramids of Teotihuacan, the baroque altars, and postmodern clones, the popular city offers its rituals and its symphonic noise. 'Bésame mucho, bésame mucho, each time I cling to your lips I hear divine music.'

On the causes for pride that (should) make one shiver

'It was written I should be loyal to the nightmare of my choice.'
Joseph Conrad, *Heart of Darkness*
'People do not live in places but in the description of places.'
Wallace Stevens.

Where has that chauvinism of old gone according to which, as the saying goes, 'There is nowhere like Mexico?' Not far, of course: it has returned as chauvinism hidden in the language of catastrophe and fatal demography. I will now enumerate some points of pride (psychological compensation):

—Mexico City is the most populated city in the world;

—México City is a polluted city, whose population, however, does not seem to want to move (the laboratory of the extinction of nomadic existence);

—Mexico is the place where it would be impossible for anything to fail due to a lack of audience. There is public aplenty. In the capital, to counterbalance the lack of clear skies, there are more than enough inhabitants, spectators, car-owners, pedestrians. Don't cry for me loneliness;

—Mexico City is the place where the unliveable has its rewards, the first of which has been to endow survival with a new status.

Mexico City is the place where, comparatively speaking, very few people actually leave or want to leave. What for? In the vital statistics (which tend, for the most part, to be short of the mark) everyone invents as they like: here Truth is always the opposite of a real confidence in truth. Real pessimism is a bag of special effects, and this is because, since it is a secular city and very much so, very few take seriously the predicted end of the world—at least, of *this* world. Doomsday, Doomsday, stay here and don't let anything happen to us. So what are the retentive powers of a megalopolis which, without a doubt, has reached its historic limit? And how do we reconcile this sense of having reached a limit, with the medium and long-term plans of every city dweller? Is it only centralist anxiety that determines the intensity of the city's hold? *And what will be the fate of our grandchildren? Well, living in the open air is so boring.*

For many, Mexico City's major charm is precisely its (true and false) status as being at the end of all beginnings. Here is the first megalopolis to fall victim to its own excess. And how fascinating are all the biblical prophecies, the dismal statistics and the joyful or sad experiences of people when they view the situation. *Listen, family, I know what you did last summer. Give me a job to build a dream on.*

The same grandiose explanation is always offered: despite the disasters, twenty or twenty-two million people *cannot leave Mexico City or the Valley of Anáhuac,*[2] *because there is nowhere else they want to go; there is nowhere else, really, that they can go.* Such resignation or such hidden joy discovers, engenders, an 'aesthetic of multitudes'. Centralism lies at the origins of the phenomenon, as does the supreme concentration of powers—which, nevertheless, has certain advantages, the first of which is the identification of liberty and tolerance: 'I don't feel like making moral judgements because then I'd have to speak to my neighbours.' Tradition is destroyed by rush hours, the replacement of the extended family by the nuclear unit, the wish for extreme individualization that accompanies anomie.

The metro (a voyage to the end of the squeeze)

Every day, almost five million people make use of Mexico City's metro, fighting a vicious battle for oxygen and millimetres. Long gone the marvellous scene of Oliver Hardy and Stan Laurel in Mexico, watching countless individuals getting out of a taxi. That was a surreal metaphor, in any case; this is something entirely different: turmoil in a nutshell. The city—its essence, its idiosyncrasies—plays itself out in the metro. Passengers are sullen or raucous, rueful or exasperated. They burst out in choral monologues or keep quiet (doubtless in an effort to communicate telepathically with their inner self). Reluctant paragons of tolerance, they boast the energy to remain upright in a stampede, to slim and instantly regain their customary body types with each squeeze. The close proximity to so many bodies breeds—and cushions—impure thoughts, and, in two or three seconds, gives impure a holy definition. In the metro, the legacy of institutionalized corruption, ecological devastation and the repression of human rights is formally passed on to each passenger and to the legions he or she potentially contains (each passenger will engender a carriage-full, in California in 2006, 52 per cent of newborns were of Hispanic origin, most of them Mexican. The invasion of the bellies, said the racist.). They keep this heritage alive: it's the 'humanism of the squeeze'.

While one cannot claim with the ancient saying that what feeds ten people will also feed eleven, one can assert that where a thousand fit, ten thousand will be crammed, for space is more fertile than food. In all the

[2] The Valley of Mexico.

13

Figure 1.2 Solidarity. Mexico City metro.
© Francisco Mata Rosas.

world, there is nothing so flexible as space; there's always room for one more, and another and another, and in the metro, human density is not a sign of the struggle for life, but of the opposite. Who said objects cannot occupy the same space at the same time? In the metro, the laws of molecular structure lose their universal validity, bodies merge like spiritual essences, and transcorporeal graftings are commonplace.

One can attain pluralism by venturing into the metro at peak hours (feats of warlike retreat, already calling for their Xenophon), or by venturing into public housing projects where privacy is a matter of weaving and dodging, an aspiration contradicted by packed streets and families breeding in front of the television set. There are so many of us that even the most outlandish thought is shared by millions. There are so many of us, who cares if the next man agrees or disagrees? There are so many of us that the real miracle is getting home, closing the front door, and seeing the crowds magically diminish.

How could one not be a pluralist, when subway trips teach us the virtues of unity in diversity? How could one not be a pluralist, when identity is constructed by pushing and shoving, and maintained by the mysteries of population explosion? Prejudices become personal views, demography takes the place of tradition, and we remember this about the past: there used to be fewer people, and the old minorities (in contrast to the current majorities) counterbalanced their numerical handicap by spending time outdoors. Claustrophobia arose—a hunger for fresh air, for a life that could never go underground and could never be compared to a descent into hell—and street life prospered. Then came the metro, and agoraphobia became fashionable.

Is it possible to score in the metro? Many say yes, it's a piece of cake, because if the metro represents the city and recreates the street, it must by necessity contain sex—all kinds of sex. Packed into subway cars, humankind reverts to primal chaos, a *horror vacui* that is fertile ground for propositions, the rubbing of bodies, lustful advances frustrated by lack of differentiation, surreptitious grinding, blatant grinding, risk taking, and other transgressions. It's all the same in the end. The metro abolishes singularity, anonymity, chastity, desire—mere individual reactions that become insignificant in the larger scale of things, in which a former 'many' is the only precedent for the current 'too many'. It's all the same whether one enters or exits. But machismo still reigns supreme.

The metro's perpetual novelty consists of concentrating the entire country into one square metre. A feat of hospitality, each carriage becomes a biblical metaphor, generating space for loners, couples, families, tribes, progenies. The metro dissolves the boundaries between bodies; there is room for everyone, after all.

You must remember this: a city is still a city

Mexico City is transforming itself architecturally to be close to the border. This is also known as Americanization, this search for resemblance to cities bordering the United States, with identical restaurants, malls that loom as bastions of abundance, movie theatres like those in San Diego or McAllen, *prêt-à-porter*, Blockbuster, McDonald's, Wal-Mart, Sears Roebuck, Tower Records. Every day, the ideal frontier is crossed, and those 'lacking roots' (the majority) realize that the roots of one's identity also defend against fads . . . up to a point.

Figure 1.3 Free Time. Mexico City metro. © Francisco Mata Rosas.

In this context, Mexico City is a frontier city par excellence. Industry, commerce and entertainment closely resemble an urban monster of twenty million people with a *borderline* appearance. Of course it fails, but in some places they achieve it, at least an illusion of walking for a couple of minutes in another city in another country that is vaguely reminiscent of scenes from certain North American movies with a Latin flavour, mixing of course memory and desire. Part of the border is captured visually and in this way consumer society satisfies its desire for travel. Without passports or dangers, Mexicans are already crossing the Río Bravo. Virtual geographic mobility.

Do not overstate the fantasy. The Border exists, with force, cruelty, racism and rejection. But the real, as important as it is, does not interfere with travellers' fantasies, those who desire illusions of contemporary life, or those who try to match what exists with what they dream about. If a computerized life and the Internet erase borders, if contemporary architecture tries to duplicate the forms of the urban edge, to 'deterritorialize' and force Mexicans to cross the border virtually, then we should accept the *frontier* condition as already existing in most of the sectors in the nation. To be *fronterizo* is to be willing to leave immediately, to come and go from one country to another in reality or the imagination, to identify the typical and traditional as repositories of nostalgia but not of reality. And with twenty million Mexicans living in the United States, somebody can sing 'North of the Border down Mexico way.'

In practice, nothing could be further from the spirit of the capital city than the prophecies contained in Carlos Fuentes's novel *Christopher Unborn* and in his short story 'The Son of Andrés Aparicio' in *Burnt Water*.[3] According to Fuentes, the city has reached its limits. One of his characters reflects:

> He was ashamed that a nation of churches and pyramids built for all eternity ended up becoming one with the cardboard, shitty city. They boxed him in, suffocated him, took his sun and air away, his senses of vision and smell.

Even the world of *Christopher Unborn* (one of ecological, political, social and linguistic desolation) is invaded by fun ('*relajo*'). In the end, although the catastrophe may be very real, catastrophism is the celebration of the incredulous in which irresponsibility mixes with resignation and hope, and in practice, optimism wins out. In the last instance, the advantages seem greater that the horrors. And the result is: *Mexico, the post-apocalyptic city*, the vanguard of the last ecology of happiness and fear, the space which all the tourists of disasters would like to visit on Judgement Day. That's of course a big lie but who knows? At the end, the witnesses would be unable to sell their chronicles.

Further Reading

Monsiváis, Carlos, *Días de guardar* (Mexico City: Ediciones Era, 1970).

———, *Amor perdido* (Mexico City: Ediciones Era, 1977).

———, *Entrada libre: Crónicas de la sociedad que se organiza* (Mexico City: Ediciones Era, 1977).

———, *Escenas de pudor y liviandad* (Mexico City: Ediciones Era, 1988).

———, *Los rituales del caos* (Mexico City: Ediciones Era, 1995).

———, *Mexican Postcards*, trans. and ed. John Kraniauskas (London: Verso, 1997).

———(ed.), *A ustedes les consta. Antología de la crónica en México* (Mexico City: Ediciones Era, 1980).

---

[3] Carlos Fuentes, *Christopher Unborn* (New York: Farrar, Straus & Giroux, 1989) and *Burnt Water* (London: Secker and Warburg, 1981).

II
HISTORY

2. THE PRE-COLUMBIAN CITY
Tenochtitlan: the First Mexico City

WARWICK BRAY

When the Spanish conquistadors entered the Aztec capital and destroyed it, an anonymous Nahuatl poet expressed the bitterness and bewilderment of a people whose gods had deserted them and whose days of glory had suddenly come to an end:

> There is nothing but grief and suffering in Mexico and Tlatelolco,
> where once we saw beauty and valour.
> Have you grown weary of your servants?
> Are you angry with your servants,
> O Giver of Life?[1]

Nearly five centuries later the Aztec kings and gods have gone, but Nahuatl is still a living language and one does not have to look very hard to see elements of Aztec Tenochtitlan in today's Mexico City—physically (in the archaeological remains of the Great Temple, the street plan of the city and the advertisements on its walls, the faces in the marketplace), but also psychologically, in the ways the Mexican people see themselves.

It is a common jibe in Latin America that the countries which most glorify the past are the ones that have no future. Mexico is emphatically *not* one of those failing countries, though here, too, the past has been politicized and to some extent co-opted by the state for its own purposes. The pre-Hispanic world makes an appearance in the ideology of revolution, the Indigenista movement, the Diego Rivera murals in the Palacio National, in essential tourist revenue from (state-controlled) archaeology, and—gloriously—in the Museum of Anthropology. The inauguration of this world-ranking museum in 1964 combined cultural and political self-assertion in a totally beneficial way.

But, although the past is inescapable in Mexico City, reconstructing Aztec Teonochtitlan is an exercise in imagination. Of the conquistadors who visited the city before its destruction, only five have left eyewitness

[1] Miguel León-Portilla (ed.), *The Broken Spears: the Aztec Account of the Conquest of Mexico* (London: Constable and Company, 1962), p. 149.

accounts. The letters that Hernán Cortés wrote to the emperor Charles V incorporate vivid descriptions of Aztec life, and these can be supplemented by the works of his companions, Bernal Díaz del Castillo, Andrés de Tapia, Francisco de Aguilar and a soldier who describes himself simply as 'a gentleman attached to Señor Fernando Cortés'. Apart from a handful of native pictorial documents (often in the form of colonial copies) all other accounts are based on the memories of old people who had seen Tenochtitlan during its days of Aztec glory. The product of churchmen, bureaucrats, lawyers and historians, both Spanish and Mestizo, these colonial documents are often accurate at the level of description but their authors, as Christians, have difficulties in grappling with the subtleties of the Aztec mind.

The loss of so much indigenous paperwork is a major tragedy. Those who have suffered from Mexican bureaucracy usually blame their frustrations on the Spanish heritage, but Mexico was a bureaucratic, literate and centralized society long before the European conquest. Ixtlilxochitl, brother of the last native ruler of Texcoco, has left this account in the prologue to his *Historia Chichimeca*:

> They had scribes for each branch of knowledge. Some dealt with the annals, putting in order the things which happened each year, giving the day, month and hour. Others had charge of the genealogies, recording the lineage of rulers, lords and noblemen, registering the newborn and deleting those who had died. Some painted the frontiers, limits and boundary markers of the cities, provinces and villages, and also the distribution of fields, whose they were and to whom they belonged. Other scribes kept the law books and those dealing with the rites and ceremonies which they practised when they were infidels. The priests recorded all matters to do with the temples and images, with their idolatrous doctrines, the festivals of their false gods and their calendars. And finally, the philosophers and learned men which there were among them were charged with painting all the sciences which they had discovered, and with teaching by memory all the songs in which were embodied their scientific knowledge and historical traditions.[2]

This passage clearly shows the impact of Christian and European values on those members of the old elite who were looking for advancement in the colonial world.

Cumulatively, the surviving paperwork provides a kaleidoscopic, but patchy and incomplete, picture of life in Tenochtitlan that allows us to put back real people into the streets of the capital. The sources also emphasize two things that an archaeologist should never forget. One is that the people

---

[2] Fernando de Alva Ixtlilxochitl, *Obras Completas*, ed. Edmundo O'Gorman (Mexico City: Universidad Nacional Autónoma, 1975), vol. 1 p. 527.

whose culture he is studying are not so very different from us; the other is that there are many different ways of running a civilization and that most of them will work. Underneath the exotic surface are many things that are familiar and that we can easily identify with today.

By any definition of the word, Mexico has been civilized for 2,000 years or more. The people we know as the Aztecs did not emerge from nowhere, but represent the final stage of a long cultural, political and technological tradition as old as anything that Christian Europe can offer.

The story of Mexico City begins in the year Two Reed (AD 1324 in our own calendar), and the events take place in a Basin of Mexico which was very different from anything the visitor sees today. The floor of the Basin was occupied by a great lake (now almost completely drained), and scattered along its shores were some fifty independent city-states of various sizes. The political setting was in many ways similar to that of Classical Greece or Renaissance Italy, and the strategies for political survival adopted by Aztec kings can all be found in Machiavelli's advice to the ruler of Florence. Many of the towns of the Aztec period still exist, and under their original names, though several of them (Coyoacan, Xochimilco, Chapultepec, Tlatelolco, Acapotzalco) have been swallowed up by modern Mexico City. Into this environment the people we know as the Aztecs were late immigrants and, inevitably, they were unwelcome and found no vacant land to occupy.

But in the year Two Reed a momentous event took place. According to their own histories, it was foretold that the Mexica (as the Aztecs called themselves) would find a home where their priests would see an eagle standing on a cactus and holding a snake in its beak. The prophecy was fulfilled in 1324, and the site was an unoccupied mud bank just offshore in Lake Texcoco. Here, at the place they called Tenochtitlan, the Aztecs settled down, and the history of Mexico City begins.

A few years later, on another muddy island only a bowshot away, the Aztecs created their second settlement at Tlatelolco. Both settlements flourished and, with the conquest of Tlatelolco by its larger neighbour after a civil war in 1473, the twin cities merged into a single great conurbation. The centre of the once-independent town of Tlatelolco has been excavated by archaeologists and is today the Plaza de las Tres Culturas. Here, in the College of Santa Cruz de Tlatelolco founded by the Franciscans for the training of Indian novices, Bernardino de Sahagún compiled his great encyclopaedia that is still the most comprehensive source on Aztec life.

Like many other historical events, the story of the eagle, the cactus and the snake may be pure invention, but the symbolic consequences are with us still. The Mexica gave their name to a vigorous modern country, and the

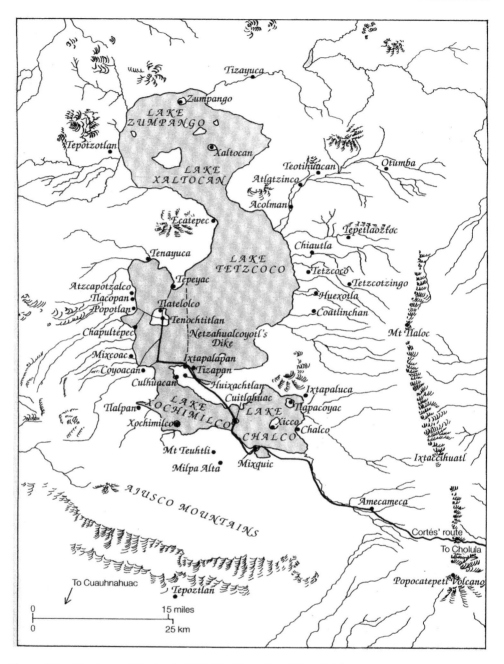

Figure 2.1 The Basin of Mexico in 1519. The island city of Tenochtitlan–Tlatelolco was linked to the mainland by causeways. Nezahualcoyotl's dike separated the salty waters of the northern lakes from the sweet water southern lakes that were the site of the *chinampas*. From Richard F. Townsend, *The Aztecs* (London: Thames and Hudson, 1992, p. 27). © Thames and Hudson.

eagle and the snake still appear everywhere—on the Mexican flag, the coinage and on the facades of government buildings in every small town.

At the time of its foundation, Tenochtitlan was just a collection of reed huts surrounding a humble temple dedicated to Huitzilopochtli, the tribal god of the Aztecs. Two hundred years later, when the Europeans arrived, it was a stone-built city, larger than any in Europe. It was also the centre of a conquest-empire. The territory controlled by the Aztecs stretched across Mexico from the Pacific to the Atlantic, and nearly 500 city-states paid taxes and tribute to the Aztec ruler and his allies. We shall see later how important these tribute goods were to the Aztec economy.

The history of Aztec Tenochtitlan is compressed into no more than two centuries and, built on a virgin site, unencumbered by earlier structures, it physically represents a piece of state-planning that reflects Aztec ideas about what a city ought to be. From reviewers' comments it is clear that visitors to the splendid Aztec exhibition at the Royal Academy in 2002–2003 came away impressed by the quality and, above all, by the strangeness and power of the items on display, but behind this exoticism there are other aspects of city life that we should think about. A capital city like Tenochtitlan is simultaneously a centre of government, religion and commerce, and it is evident from the documentary sources that its authorities had to deal with the sorts of problems we are all too familiar with: how to control crime and administer justice, how to provide clean water and enough food for the inhabitants, how to distribute this food and other goods, how to remove waste, educate children, tackle urban growth and migration to the city, how to collect taxes, carry out public works, and so on. Although the Aztec capital *looked* quite unlike any European city, *in functional terms* it was not very different from sixteenth-century Madrid or twenty-first century London.

That said, we can begin to reconstruct imperial Tenochtitlan. Since most of it is buried under Mexico City, in practice this means re-creating the city by an exercise of imagination, based on Spanish and indigenous documents and on limited archaeological evidence from the pre-Hispanic centre. On best estimates the city covered about 12 square kilometres and had between 200,000 and 300,000 inhabitants. This huge population growth is impossible to explain away by natural increase of the original Aztec founders, so we must think in terms of massive immigration from the surrounding territory and from all parts of the empire. There are hints of this in a comment by the sixteenth-century Spanish Dominican historian Diego Durán:

> the city began to fill with people from neighbouring towns and from other nations, and the Aztecs frequently joined with these people in marriage. Thus the Mexican nation multiplied and the city expanded . . . In this way they

won over the people of Tezcoco and of all towns they could convince of their goodwill. They treated travellers and strangers well; they invited merchants to come to the markets of Mexico-Tenochtitlan with their goods, for such commerce always enriches a city.[3]

To some extent Tenochtitlan must have been multicultural and multiethnic, with Nahuatl serving as a lingua franca.

From its origin, Tenochtitlan was an island city, connected to the lake shore by causeways, and with a pair of aqueducts bringing clean water from a spring at Chapultepec on the mainland. A dam 15 kilometres long, built by the ruler of nearby Texcoco, prevented the salty water of the northern lake from polluting the sweet water of the south, and also helped to control the flooding that was a problem well into the colonial era. And, like Venice, Tenochtitlan was a canal city, with waterways reaching into all parts of it. The anonymous companion of Cortés has left this description:

> The great city . . . has many broad streets, though among these are two or three pre-eminent. Of the remainder, half of each one is of hard earth like a pavement, and the other half is by water, so that they leave in their canoes, which are of wood hollowed out. The inhabitants go for a stroll, some in canoes and others along the land, and keep up conversations. Besides these are other streets entirely of water, and all travel is by canoes . . . and without these they could neither leave their houses nor return to them, and all the other towns, being on the lake, are established in the same way.[4]

Goods as well as people moved by canoe, and canoes also removed the waste from public latrines for use as fertilizer and for tanning leather. These urban canals have long been filled in, but they (and the causeways) are still recognizable in the street plan of modern Mexico City.

We can visualize the city as a series of concentric zones. In the centre, on the original island, were the royal palaces, major temples and the administrative buildings of the Aztec state. Further out, but still on dry land, were the suburbs occupied by lesser officials and ordinary people, most of whom did not engage in farming. Further out still was the city's agricultural fringe.

Pre-European Mexico was rich in plant foods but poor in domestic animals. Farmers raised turkeys and ducks, edible dogs, and little black stingless bees that provided both honey and wax, but the horses, cattle, pigs, sheep, goats and chickens that are such a prominent feature of the rural

---

[3] Diego Durán, *The History of the Indies of New Spain,* trans. Doris Heyden (Norman: University of Oklahoma Press, 1994), p. 64.
[4] *Narrative of Some Things of New Spain and of the Great City of Temestitan, Mexico,* trans. Marshall H. Saville (Boston: Longwood Press, 1978), p. 63.

landscape today were all European introductions, as were ploughs and wheeled vehicles. When the Aztec country-dweller ate meat, it was normally the flesh of game animals such as deer, rabbit, armadillo or iguana.

Salt was extracted from the saline waters of the northern lakes, and the lake system as a whole provided fish and water creatures, wildfowl, edible algae, willows for basketry, and reeds for thatching and for weaving mats. An early colonial map of 1523–5, the *Plano en Papel de Maguey*, is full of pictorial vignettes of life in the lakeside suburbs, with wickerwork traps and fish weirs set in shallow water, nets suspended from poles to catch wild birds, and representations of men in dugout canoes fishing with rods, nets and three-pointed spears. Another famous manuscript, the *Codex Mendoza*, has a page devoted to the training of young children, in which a father teaches his teenage son to catch fish and cut reeds, while a mother shows her daughter how to make tortillas and to weave on a back strap loom of the kind still used in villages all over Mexico today.

Despite the richness of the lake, the original island lacked essential resources, with no arable land, no stone or wood for building, no metals or obsidian for tool-making, no cotton for clothing, and none of the tropical luxuries that the aristocracy came to enjoy. To create farmland, the Aztecs embarked on a programme of land reclamation in the reed beds around the island. They cut canals through the marshes, and between these canals they heaped up aquatic plants. On top of this vegetation they spread fertile mud from the lake bottom, then consolidated the reclaimed plots by planting trees and by reinforcing the sides with wickerwork hurdles. These plots are called *chinampas,* and they are some of the most productive gardens in the world. They can be hand-irrigated with water from the lake and, as soon as fertility begins to decline, all that is needed is another dressing with organic mud. By using nursery beds and transplantation, and by juggling the sowing and harvesting seasons of different crops, *chinampas* can be made to produce food throughout the year, with no fallow period. It is therefore not surprising that many of today's Latin American governments are looking at the possibility of introducing *chinampa* technology in their own wetlands.

The Aztec *chinampas* were arranged in a grid of long, narrow cultivated strips separated by canals. A small corner of this landscape remains today at the popular resort of Xochimilco where, alongside the canal boats and *mariachi* bands, is a functioning Aztec landscape where the traditional techniques of gardening are still employed. Old air photographs of the drained lake bed, taken before the massive spread of Mexico City, show a corduroy pattern made up of thousands of hectares of former *chinampas*, and archaeology has confirmed that most of them are of Aztec age.

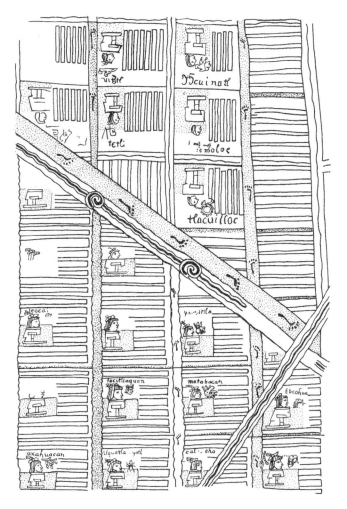

Figure 2.2 Part of an early sixteenth-century map showing the *chinampa* area. The *chinampa* strips are separated by narrow canals, and the house of each owner stands on a patch of solid land. Major canals are indicated by wavy lines and curly symbols, and canal-side streets by rows of footprints. Courtesy of Warwick Bray.

We have sixteenth-century documents, too. Figure 2.2 shows part of a land map with about 400 *chinampa* properties. Each one has its strips of farmland, the house of the owner, and even his name in Aztec glyphs and Spanish alphabetic writing. A series of legal documents, studied by Edward Calnek, gives the ownership history of individual *chinampa* plots from pre-conquest to early colonial times, and many of these properties can still be located on the street map of Mexico City. The documents give the exact size and shape of each holding, with ground plans of the buildings and an indication of whether the *chinampas* were within the city of Tenochtitlan or lay outside it. This information gives us not only the size and boundaries of the Aztec capital, and a means for estimating its population, but also a glimpse of the layout of the agricultural suburbs. Unlike the larger map, which represents an area outside Tenochtitlan, the urban plans show house lots fronting on a street, with *chinampa* strips at the back, running down to a canal. On the other side of this canal the pattern was repeated as a mirror image, first the *chinampas*, then the house with its street entrance beyond.

Because the technology is much the same today, once we know the total area under cultivation we can work out the productivity of the *chinampa* zone. Depending on whose calculations one follows, it would have provided between one-fifth and one-half of the city's food requirements. With a shortfall of 50 per cent or more, the importance of tribute in the form of food from the conquered territories becomes very obvious.

Within the ring of *chinampa* suburbs is the dry land of the original island—though 'dry' is something of a misnomer. Deep below Mexico City, in the Aztec strata under the colonial buildings, are huge numbers of wooden piles driven in to consolidate the soft land and to alleviate the subsidence that is still a problem today. The suburbs of Tenochtitlan lie underneath Mexico City, and we know less about this zone than we do about the centre and the periphery, but ever since colonial times there have been sporadic, accidental, discoveries of Aztec building foundations and artefacts. These include some of the most iconic museum pieces, such as the great statue of Coatlicue (the Earth Mother) and the Calendar Stone, both of them found at the Plaza Mayor in 1790. More recently we have the round temple, dedicated to Ehecatl the Wind God, which is now preserved in the Pino Suárez metro station, and an overwhelming mass of material from the excavation of the metro tunnels.

Documents tell us that for administrative purposes the city was divided into four Great Quarters, and these in turn were subdivided into a number of *calpullis*, roughly equivalent to Hispanic barrios or English parishes, with some political responsibilities at local level. There is debate about whether or not the *calpullis* were kin groups of related families, but above all they were landowning corporations. Land was owned communally by the *calpulli*, which assigned plots to individual families. Each *calpulli* had its own headman, its local temple and school, and raised its own contingent of men for the army. Some *calpullis* were made up of farming families, but in the more urban zone there were *calpullis* of specialist tradesmen such as merchants, goldsmiths and feather workers.

To get an idea of what the house of an ordinary family looked like, we must supplement documentary evidence by reference to excavation at rural sites that have not yet been destroyed by the expansion of Mexico City. Buildings in Tenochtitlan were normally single storey, and only the most important had a second floor. Walls were of stone, adobe or cane, depending on the status of the owner, and roofs were either thatched or else flat and supported by beams. Documents tell us that most house compounds were occupied by several related families, often parents and married children, and that single-family residence was unusual. As the composition of the extended family changed from one generation to another, new buildings were added and old ones modified in a continuous process of adjustment.

One of the features that amazed the conquistadors for its size and variety was the Great Market at Tlatelolco. In one of his letters Hernán Cortés wrote: 'There is also one square twice as large as the city of Salamanca, surrounded by arcades where more than 60,000 souls come each day to buy and sell.'[5] All trade was by barter, though cacao beans served as a form of currency, and, as in Mexican markets today, each commodity had its own subsection. Certain local markets were famous for their specialities: Acolman for edible dogs, Azcapotzalco for birds and slaves, Cholula for featherwork and pottery, and Texcoco for its textiles and painted gourds. The market at Tlatelolco was on an altogether different scale. Here, all the products of the empire were on sale; basic items like raw and cooked food, wooden beams, reed mats, baskets, pots, salt, clothing, medicines, paper, paint, and so on, and also imported luxury goods: gold jewellery and quills filled with gold dust, turquoise and jade, jaguar skins, tropical feathers, rubber and cacao (cocoa) beans. Bernal Díaz, who has left a detailed description, commented that the noise of the market could be heard as far away as the Great Temple.

State bureaucracy stretched from the palace to the marketplace, and Tlatelolco market was under the direct control of the Aztec ruler. Pedlars and stallholders paid a fee to the market superintendent, and inspectors mingled with the crowds, checking the quality of the merchandise and making sure that prices were not too high. False measures were destroyed, and any trader passing off shoddy goods had his stock confiscated. Thieves and sellers of stolen property were tried on the spot, and convicted thieves were beaten to death in the marketplace where they had committed their crimes. The same court dealt with disputes between traders.

At the heart of Tenochtitlan were the major buildings of the Aztec state, the palaces of successive rulers, the principal temples and aristocratic residences. This is the area that the Spanish levelled and took over for their own purposes—what is now the Zócalo and the historic centre of

[5] Hernán Cortés, *Cartas y documentos*, ed. Mario Hernández Sánchez-Barba (Mexico: Editorial Porrúa, 1963), p. 72.

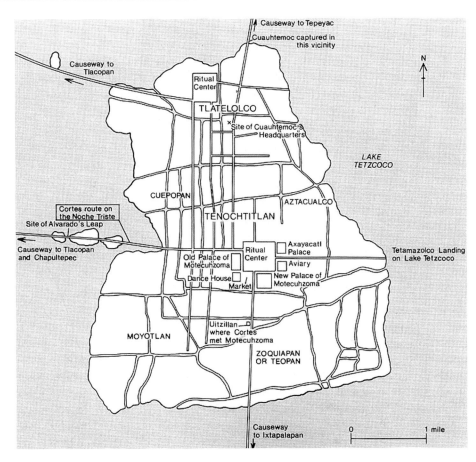

Figure 2.3 Schematic map of Tenochtitlan–Tlatelco showing the four Great Quarters (Cuepopan, Atzacualco, Moyotlan, Teopan), the main canals and streets, and the principal buildings. From Richard F. Townsend, *The Aztecs* (London: Thames and Hudson, 1992), p. 29). © Thames and Hudson.

Mexico City. Within the Aztec centre the Great Temple has recently been excavated, but most of the rest remains inaccessible below colonial and recent buildings.

The royal palaces were large. Cortés lodged his entire force in just one of the older palaces, and it is recorded that Moctezuma's 'New Palace' had a single hall capable of holding 3,000 people. This New Palace occupied a site 200 metres on each side, and served both as the ruler's private residence and the administrative hub of the empire. This dual function is reflected in its architecture. The building was set in a garden, with its own aviary and zoo. It is said to have had three courtyards, and from a drawing in the *Codex Mendoza* we know that it was arranged on two levels or terraces. On the upper floor were the apartments of Moctezuma and his household, and the ground floor was given over to administration and public works. It contained a council hall, appeal court, the state treasury and the storehouses where tribute was kept. There was also an oratory, a hall for music and dancing, quarters for 3,000 servants and palace craftsmen, a jail, an arsenal, and guest rooms for ambassadors and important visitors. The Anonymous Conqueror, who had the opportunity to explore the building, commented: 'I walked until I was tired, and never saw the whole of it.' The royal palace in the neighbouring city of Texcoco was equally grand, with more than 300 rooms. Its upkeep absorbed the tribute labour of forty-two villages and, it is recorded, 1,000 turkeys were sent to its kitchens every day. A sketch of the palace of Nezahualcoyotl, poet-king of Texcoco, depicts a throne room, a place for storing warriors' equipment, judges' quarters, store rooms for tribute, and a hall for music and science, indicated by an upright drum and a conch shell trumpet.

At the very centre of Tenochtitlan, where the city's major avenues converged, was the Great Precinct, a complex of religious buildings surrounded by a wall decorated with serpents. Inside the wall were temples, quarters for the priests, a ball court, and a skull rack, where the heads of sacrificed victims were displayed on cross-poles. One chronicler estimated that there were 62,000 heads on the rack. Andrés de Tapia gives an even higher figure and explains how he arrived at it:

> The writer and a certain Gonzalo de Umbria counted the cross sticks which were stretched from pole to pole, as I have described, and multiplying by five skulls per cross piece we found there to be 136,000 heads, without those of the towers.[6]

The towers he mentions were constructed of skulls cemented with lime mortar. Archaeologists have found part of an actual skull rack at Tlatelolco, with rows of human skulls, perforated at each temple, aligned on now-disintegrated wooden poles, and at Tenochtitlan itself a stone platform base, carved with rows of skulls, has been excavated in the Great Precinct close to the Templo Mayor. In this same area there was also the gladiatorial stone to which captives were tethered and made to fight with a succession of warriors until the prisoners were killed.

The naive and simplified plan of the Great Precinct in Figure 2.4 comes from Bernardino de Sahagún's *Codex Florentino*, and was compiled from memory after the Spanish had cleared the area for their own buildings. There were, in fact, many more Aztec structures than appear on the plan.

[6] *Colección de documentos para la historia de Mexico*, ed. Joaquin García Icazbalceta (Mexico, 1866), vol. 2, p. 583.

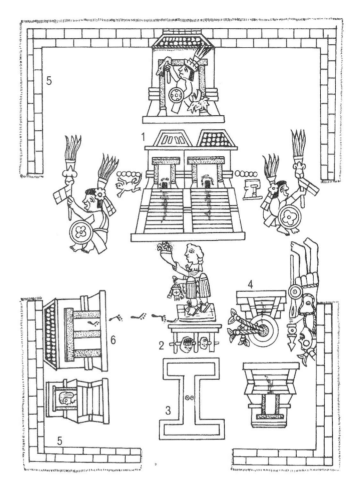

Figure 2.4 Bernardino de Sahagún's plan of the Great Precinct of Tenochtitlan. 1. Great Temple, with shrines of Huitzilopochtli and Tlaloc; 2. Skull rack; 3. Ball court; 4. Stone for gladiatorial sacrifice; 5. Serpent wall; 6. Priest's quarters. Courtesy of Warwick Bray.

One was a temple dedicated to Quetzalcoatl, the Feathered Serpent, of which Bernal Díaz has left us an eyewitness description:

> One of its doors was in the form of a most terrible mouth, such as they paint to depict the doors of hell. This mouth was open and contained great fangs to devour souls. By the side of the door were groups of devils, and forms shaped like the bodies of serpents, and a little way off was a place of sacrifice, all bloodstained and black with dried blood.[7]

[7] Bernal Díaz del Castillo, *The Conquest of New Spain*, trans. John M. Cohen (Harmondsworth: Penguin Books, 1963), p. 239.

33

Díaz also remarked that the place smelled worse than a slaughterhouse in Spain.

Dominating the whole area was the Great Temple, an immense platform in the shape of a tiered pyramid topped by twin temples (Figures 2.4 and 2.5). One was dedicated to Huitzilopochtli (god of war, and patron of the Aztecs), the other to Tlaloc, god of the rain that fertilized the land. Politically and symbolically the Great Temple brought together the two pillars of the Aztec state—the warrior elite (whose activities brought wealth and tribute) and the farmers who kept everybody fed.

The Great Temple was also the focal point of a sacred landscape, a network of localities that extended outwards into the Basin of Mexico and played an important role in the ritual cycle of the state religion. The hill of Huixachtlan, an extinct volcano between lakes Texcoco and Xochimilco, was the scene of the New Fire Ceremony that took place at the end of each fifty-two-year calendar cycle when it was feared that the sun would fail to rise and the world would come to an end. The sign that the world was safe for another fifty-two years was the rising of the constellation of the 'fire drill', probably Orion's belt, on the western horizon. At that moment a man was sacrificed on the platform at Huixachtlan, a fire drill placed in his opened chest, and a new fire kindled. From these sparks a bonfire was lit on the hill, and runners with pine torches carried the sacred flame to relight the temple hearths in the barrios of Tenochtitlan. Another temple, on Mount Tlaloc, above the tree line, was the scene of an annual pilgrimage made by the rulers of Tenochtitlan, Texcoco, Tlacopan and Xochimilco to call forth rain at the height of the dry season. Other shrines were located at the hill of Tetzcotzingo.

Symbolically, as well as politically, the city of Tenochtitlan was the hub of a wider world, but everything, eventually, leads back to the city's Great Temple, the axis mundi of the Aztec universe. The temple platform covered an area the size of a modern city block and was enlarged several times under successive rulers, leaving the earlier temples inside, like a nest of Chinese boxes. Nearly everything was removed by the Spanish, and the stones recycled into their own buildings, but the earliest (and smallest) Aztec temple is below the colonial ground level and is fairly well preserved, with its double staircase and the lower parts of the two shrines.

The Great Temple was the scene of important religious events and sacrifices, and was the burial place of rulers, but it was also a piece of symbolic architecture, glorifying in stone the Aztec state and its gods. Some scholars (notably Eduardo Matos Moctezuma) consider that the various tiers of the pyramid represent the layers of the Aztec universe, and that the orientation has religious and astronomical significance. I am sceptical about some of this, but more convinced by the argument that the Temple is a

Figure 2.5   View of the Zócalo with a photomontage of the Templo Mayor. From *Les Aztèques: Les trésors du Mexique ancien*, Exhibition Catalogue Musées Royaux d'Art et d'Histoire, Brussels 1987. © Musées Royaux d'Art et d'Histoire.

manifestation of the Aztec creation myths and the story of the birth of Huitzilopochtli.

These events took place at Coatepec, the Hill of the Snake. For the Aztecs, the temple pyramid *was* Coatepec, a representation in stone of one of the key events in Aztec mythology. Serpent imagery is everywhere. According to the myth, when the Earth Goddess became pregnant with Huitzilopochtli (in very dubious circumstances) her other children, egged on by the Moon Goddess, decided to kill the infant at birth. But Huitzilopochtli was born fully formed, and with the help of a Fire Serpent he killed all his siblings, chopped up the Moon Goddess, and threw the pieces down the hill. Just as we have it in the story, Huitzilopochtli sits in triumph at the top of Coatepec hill, and at the bottom of the staircase, directly below him, was found a huge round stone depicting the Moon Goddess, dressed in full regalia but with the head and limbs severed from her body. It was the accidental discovery of this monument in 1978 that triggered the full excavation of the Templo Mayor.

The symbolic nature of the Great Temple extended below ground level, and the pyramid's foundations contained buried offering-caches with thousands of artefacts. The selection and arrangement of these items was not random, but was designed to reinforce the message of the temple structure. Two themes predominate: water (Tlaloc) and conquest (Huitzilopochtli). Water-related objects include little vessels with the face mask of Tlaloc, model canoes with fishing equipment, sea sand, marine shells from both the Atlantic and the Pacific Oceans, coral, miniature fish made from mother of pearl, and the skeletons of fish, water birds, turtles and crocodiles. The warrior element is represented by trophy objects from conquered provinces in the modern states of Guerrero, Oaxaca, Puebla and Veracruz. Other items in the caches were heirlooms from the earlier Olmec and Teotihuacan civilizations, and they allude to the Aztecs' view of themselves as the rightful heirs to these past empires. Once buried, these objects were never seen again. Although invisible to the public, and making no visual impact, their presence was part of the very essence of the Temple.

It was the excavation of the Templo Mayor that produced some of the most spectacular items in recent exhibitions. What these new finds from the Great Precinct have done, because of their fine preservation, is put back the colour into our image of the Aztec capital. Like the central zones of our own cities, the public spaces of Tenochtitlan were filled with sculptures and murals celebrating the state, its rulers and their conquests, and the gods who made their success possible. It was propaganda art, as state art always is, whether civil or religious. Recent excavations at the 'Eagle House' (the meeting-house of one of the Aztec warrior orders) give some idea of how the Great Precinct would have looked in its prime. Platform bases with eagle mouldings gave access to a series of inner rooms arranged round two open patios. From this area came two life-size clay sculptures of warriors wearing eagle costumes with the remains of stucco and white paint on the feathers. These figures stood on polychrome benches, carved and painted with images of armed warriors marching towards a ball of straw studded with the implements used to draw blood in the act of self-sacrifice. These friezes are direct copies of benches at Tula, the capital of the former Toltec empire. Nothing in the 'Eagle House' was purely decorative. With every glance the warriors were confronted with overlapping references to war, imperial glory, blood and sacrifice.

Outdoors, too, public sculptures were painted, and the facades of buildings were faced with gleaming stucco painted with scenes, deities, or simple blocks of colour. To complete the picture we have to imagine the squares filled with people in multicoloured clothing. Add to this the noise, the smells of flowers, blood and sweat, and my re-imagined Tenochtitlan is very different from the monochrome world of old fashioned Aztec sculpture galleries.

This chapter began by looking at the Aztec capital in *functional terms,* as a working city, and has ended up by examining it as a *symbolic artefact*. Of course it was both those things but, transformed into a political and cultural symbol of a rather different kind, Tenochtitlan has become embedded in the national consciousness of modern Mexico, and into the way that Mexicans define themselves.

Further Reading

Boone, Elizabeth Hill (ed.), *The Aztec Templo Mayor* (Washington: Dumbarton Oaks Research Library & Collection, 1987).

Díaz del Castillo, Bernal, *The Conquest of New Spain*, trans. John M. Cohen (Harmondsworth: Penguin, 1963).

Matos Moctezuma, Eduardo, *The Great Temple of the Aztecs: Treasures of Tenochtitlan* (London: Thames & Hudson, 1988).

The Royal Academy of Arts, *Aztecs* (Exhibition Catalogue, November 2002–April 2003) (London: Royal Academy of Arts, 2002).

Townsend, Richard F., *The Aztecs* (London: Thames & Hudson, 1992).

3. THE COLONIAL CITY
Imperial Mexico: the Viceregal Capital
D. A. BRADING

For three hundred years the city of Mexico was the capital of a vast viceroyalty that eventually stretched from Honduras to California and which actively supported the Spanish presence in the Philippines and the Caribbean. After the three-month siege of Tenochtitlan, Hernán Cortés sought permission to call the conquered land New Spain and boldly informed Charles V, that 'Your highness . . . may call himself once more emperor, with a title and with no less merit than that of Germany, which through the grace of God your sacred Majesty possesses.'[1] Three years later, after his return from Honduras, in 1524 Cortés welcomed the arrival of the Franciscan mission to New Spain, kneeling in the dust before the assembled nobility, both Spanish and Aztec, to kiss the hand of Martín de Valencia, the leader of the twelve travel-stained friars who had walked barefoot from Veracruz. In his last letter to the emperor, the conqueror remarked on the success which had greeted this mission, since the Indians had flocked to hear their message. He exclaimed: 'in a very short time we can take it for certain that a new Church will arise, where more than in any other part of the world Our Lord will be honoured and served'.[2]

It was Hernán Cortés who chose to pitch the capital of New Spain amidst the ruins of Tenochtitlan, albeit calling it by its second Nahua name of Mexico. The contrast with Peru is remarkable, since Francisco Pizarro ignored Cuzco, the Inca capital, and built a Spanish city in Lima, close to the Pacific coast. Moreover, Cortés converted the ceremonial centre of Tenochtitlan, where all the temples were concentrated, into a great open square that came to be called the Zócalo. So too, he constructed a substantial building that was later to become the viceregal palace on the very site of Moctezuma's palace and gardens. But he made no attempt to demolish what remained of the Templo Mayor, the great pyramid-temple that still soared over the city, wishing to preserve it as testimony of former grandeur.

---

[1] Hernán Cortés, *Cartas y documentos*, ed. Mario Hernández Sánchez-Barba (Mexico: Editorial Porrúa, 1963), p. 33.
[2] *Ibid.*, p. 318.

In this context, it should be remembered that Cortés always averred that Moctezuma had paid homage to Charles V, summoning the Mexican nobility to follow suit, so that a peaceful cession of sovereignty, a *translatio imperii*, had occurred. The subsequent Aztec resistance was hence an act of rebellion. In effect, viceregal Mexico was thus presented as the legitimate successor state to Tenochtitlan. In later years, the first great church historian of New Spain, Jerónimo de Mendieta, depicted Cortés as a Moses who had led the peoples of Anáhuac out of the Egypt of idolatry into the Promised Land of the Christian Church.

By all accounts, it was Antonio de Mendoza, the first viceroy (1534–50), who launched a concerted attempt to create a Spanish city and endow it with a range of appropriate institutions. The scion of a powerful noble family, the son of the first viceroy of Granada after the capture of that Muslim city in 1492, he had served in Italy as a diplomat and was familiar with the literature and art of the Renaissance. It was his decision, taken in 1538, to destroy the Templo Mayor and level the remaining Aztec edifices in order to create a great central square from which there radiated in chequer-board design the colonial city. To guide him, Mendoza consulted Leon Battista Alberti's *De re aedificatoria* (1485), a copy of which he possessed, albeit of the 1512 Paris edition. But he also was familiar with Santa Fe, the Spanish town in Granada that had been laid out according to the rectangular design of Roman military encampments. Moreover, the Aztec island-city had been penetrated by broad waterways, serviced by canoes, which offered a further precedent. Whatever the precedent or rationale, Mexico City was endowed with broad avenues that ran in straight lines to its limits. For all that, the decision to build the capital on an island little better than a mud flat, situated in a lake with waters constantly replenished by rivers and other lakes situated within the central basin, was to cause problems of flooding and subsidence that continue to the present day.

Mexico City was not merely the capital of New Spain, it was also the seat of the metropolitan archbishopric of Mexico. The first incumbent, Juan de Zumárraga, a zealous and learned Franciscan, was appointed bishop in 1528 and consecrated as archbishop in 1546. He readily collaborated with Mendoza and they jointly approved the foundation in 1536 of the College of Santa Cruz de Tlatelolco, administered by the Franciscans and designed to provide an education for the sons of the native nobility. The more talented were taught Latin. Although the expectation that some pupils might proceed to the priesthood proved illusory, nevertheless, a few actively collaborated with the friars in their study and interpretation of native religion, language and history. Others served as governors of their respective communities and thus acted as intermediaries between the colonial regime and the native population. Equally important, it was Zumárraga who brought over to Mexico Juan Cromberger to manage the first printing press in the New World. The first title was published in 1539 and was a compendium of Christian doctrine set out in both Spanish and *lengua mexicana*, which is to say, in Nahuatl. By 1600 over 120 titles had been printed and apart from catechisms, sermons and doctrinal treatises included a number of grammars and dictionaries of leading native languages. These Mexican incunabula constituted a unique cultural achievement and depended upon the intimate collaboration of the mendicant clergy and their native disciples. When the most learned and able of these native disciples, Antonio Valeriano, died in 1605, Franciscan friars carried his coffin into the chapel where he was to be buried; an able Latinist, he had assisted Bernardino de Sahagún in the composition of his *Historia de las cosas de Nueva España*, the greatest and most complete bilingual study of Nahua culture; he also served for thirty years as governor of the native community of Mexico City.

Prior to his departure for Peru, Mendoza added his voice to the representations of the city council of Mexico and the religious orders for the Crown to endow the capital with a university. In 1551 the foundation of the Royal and Pontifical University of Mexico was authorized by Prince Philip, acting for Charles V and on 3 June 1553 the first lectures were offered. The orator who spoke at the formal inauguration was Francisco Cervantes de Salazar, a classical scholar who taught rhetoric and a self-styled disciple of the Spanish humanist, Juan Luis Vives. The following year, Cervantes de Salazar, who was the cousin of the wealthy and devout silver-miner Alonso de Villaseca, published three Latin dialogues written to celebrate both the university and the city. Among his colleagues, he counted Alonso de la Veracruz, an Augustinian friar and a highly respected theologian, who lectured at his order's university college of San Pablo. In conversational form, Cervantes de Salazar marvelled at the width and order of the great avenues of Mexico, which had channels of water running down their centres, designed to carry off urban waste. These streets were lined with impressive palaces that were so sturdily built that they resembled fortresses. He also noted the great host of artisans and petty traders that filled the markets, where a great variety of local fruits and vegetables were brought into the centre of the city by Indians in their canoes. He also cited Valeriano as an example of Indian attainments and praised Francisco de Bustamante, a Franciscan, for his striking sermons. About his only criticism was that the city lacked a cathedral worthy of its status as a capital. Cervantes de Salazar remained in Mexico until his death and became both a canon of the cathedral and rector of the university.

When the Jesuits arrived in Mexico City in 1571, they were warmly welcomed, since by then they had acquired a reputation as admirable schoolmasters. Both the current viceroy, Martín Enríquez, and the city council greeted them enthusiastically because young Spaniards born in Mexico desperately needed 'masters of reading and writing, of Latin and other sciences'. As a Jesuit historian later explained, the mendicant orders had primarily dedicated themselves to the conversion and instruction of the native population, with the result that 'gentlemen and persons of quality' found it difficult to encounter a good education for their offspring. And yet, without such a formation, how could young Creoles, the Spaniards born in the New World, qualify as priests or lawyers, still less aspire to become canons in the cathedral chapters or judges in the high courts? It was to satisfy these aspirations that the first Jesuit provincial, Pedro Sánchez, who had lectured at the University of Salamanca, moved rapidly to establish the College of San Pedro y San Pablo in the capital, with the aim of instructing the future candidates for the priesthood. Several schools for boys were also set up which were later combined to form the College of San Ildefonso. Not content to restrict the Society to Mexico City, Sánchez toured the provinces, with the result that colleges were soon founded in all the leading cities of the viceroyalty. To maintain their churches and colleges, at the outset the Jesuits relied on donations. In Mexico City, Alonso de Villaseca gave them an entire block of land within the capital and a handsome donation of silver. When asked for advice about where to invest their monies, he advised them to purchase and develop haciendas, and so diligently did the Jesuits apply his counsel that within a few decades they became the owners of an entire chain of large estates.

During the first decades of the seventeenth century, a generation of young Creoles entered both the secular priesthood and the religious orders and united together to challenge the predominance of European Spaniards, both in the cathedral chapters and in the cloisters. Moreover, when exposed to the denigration of the Europeans, they hotly affirmed their own talents and identity. So also, they took pride in their Mexican patria, their homeland. In 1623 a Creole poet, Arias de Villalobos, saluted the entrance of a new viceroy by addressing his native city as:

> Rome of the New World in a golden century
> Venice in form, a Tyre in wealth
> In artifice a Corinth, a Cairo in trade . . .
> Athens in knowledge, in treasure a Thebes
> In you, new city of Charles V
> A new Venice, we find a new Athens.[3]

---

[3] *Documentos inéditos o muy raros para la historia de México*, vol. 12, ed. Genaro García and Carlos Pereyra (Mexico: Vda. De C. Bouret, 1907), p. 181.

But it was a Spanish-born poet, Bernardo de Balbuena, who in his *Grandeza mexicana* (1604), celebrated the beauty of the city's women, the brio and verve of its horsemen, the splendour of its churches and convents, the sanctity of its religious, and the prudence and wisdom of its magistrates. In harmonious, attractive verse, he evoked the island-city, surrounded by the waters of the lake, encircled by mountains, its landscape illumined by the transparent air of its ever-blue sky. The fortunate inhabitants of 'this Mexican paradise', so he claimed, passed the year enjoying 'an eternal spring'. Here were images that were to haunt the imagination of future generations of Mexicans.

In 1629, however, civic pride came close to despair when, after heavy rainfall, the city lay submerged, with lake water flooding its streets for four long years. Canoes were the only means of transport. Although partial flooding of the city had occurred earlier in the century, the magnitude and duration of this crisis was such that the authorities in Madrid commanded the current viceroy to convoke a great junta of citizens and institutions to discuss the desirability of shifting the entire site of the city to higher ground. But by then, so it was explained, the city already encompassed fifteen nunneries, eight hospitals, six colleges, seven convents of the male religious orders, the cathedral, two parishes, the palaces of the viceroy and archbishop, the Inquisition, prisons, the university, and city council: from whence would come the financial resources and, owing to the fall in Indian population, the labour to rebuild all these institutions elsewhere? As a result the decision taken was to draft as many Indians as possible to cut an open trench at Huehuetoca to drain off the waters of Lake Zumpango. Already a tunnel had been constructed there, but it had become blocked by falling earth. Although the repair of the tunnel and a draft of 3,000 Indians to extend the open trench were undertaken, the city continued to be exposed to flooding, albeit never on the scale it suffered in 1629 to 1634.

To provide spiritual consolation, in 1629 the archbishop brought the holy image of Our Lady of Guadalupe from her sanctuary and placed it on the high altar of the cathedral, there to remain until the floods receded. There was nothing unusual in this act, since on several occasions Our Lady of Los Remedios had been carried from her shrine to the cathedral with great pomp, albeit in this case to precipitate with prayer the arrival of long-delayed seasonal rainfall. But whereas Los Remedios was a small saddle-image brought over by a conqueror from Spain, La Guadalupana had been painted by an Indian artist in 1556 and placed in a small chapel or hermitage at Tepeyac, situated between a hill and the beginning of the main causeway that led into Mexico City. Devotion to the image steadily grew and in 1624 a new, more extensive sanctuary was completed. As the floods subsided, so devotion increased and the image was regarded as both

43

miraculous and peculiarly Mexican. In 1648 the Creole elite was thrilled to read the *Imagen de la Virgen María, Madre de Dios de Guadalupe*, in which Miguel Sánchez, a learned and pious priest, averred that the Mexican image was the exact likeness of the Woman of the Apocalypse, described in chapter twelve, and invited readers to contemplate this identity 'in the image of heaven by prophecy and, in the image of earth, the copy by miracle'.[4] Moreover, he cited 'the common, uniform and general tradition of the miracle' that in 1531 the Virgin Mary had appeared to the poor Indian called Juan Diego as he walked past the hill of Tepeyac and commanded him to inform the archbishop of Mexico, Juan de Zumárraga, that she wished to have a chapel built at Tepeyac, 'in which to show myself a merciful Mother to you and yours, to those devoted to me and to those who seek me in their necessities'. When the archbishop demurred, wanting proof, Juan Diego was instructed to gather flowers from Tepeyac in his cloak, and when he presented them to the archbishop his humble cloak was seen to bear the likeness of the Mexican Virgin. The image was thus taken to be heaven-sent, a perpetual miracle, an ark of the covenant that henceforth existed between the Mexican people and the Virgin Mary. In the century that followed the publication of Sánchez's book, devotion to La Guadalupana spread across New Spain and chapels dedicated to her cult were constructed in all the leading cities. Between 1695 and 1709 the existing sanctuary was destroyed and replaced by the impressive basilica that still stands at Tepeyac.

The corporate splendour of seventeenth-century Mexico can best be observed in *Llanto de Occidente* (1666), written by Isidro Sariñana, later to become bishop of Oaxaca, to commemorate the public exequies of the death of Philip IV of Spain. After the dignitaries entered the palace to pay their respects to the vicereine, the alter ego of the widowed queen, a vast procession wound its way through the streets and around the great square before entering the cathedral. It was headed by sixteen confraternities of Blacks, Mulattos, Chinos and Tarascan Indians, followed by the governors and officers of eighty-two Indian communities and confraternities of both the capital and from seven leagues around the city. Then came nineteen confraternities of Spaniards listed by name and the lay third orders, followed by the students of the colleges of San Ramón, San Ildefonso, Todos Santos and Cristo. The massed ranks of the religious orders followed, each individual with a candle in hand, who in all numbered 1,076 men. The arch-

---

[4] Miguel Sánchez, *Imagen de la Virgen María, Madre de Dios de Guadalupe*, reprinted in *Testimonios históricos guadalupanos*, ed. Ernesto de la Torre Villar and Ramiro Navarro de Anda (Mexico: Fondo de Cultura Económica, 1982), pp. 158–62.

confraternity of the holy sacrament preceded the cathedral chapter and its musicians, followed by the secular clergy of the city, which including the parish priests and chapter, in all numbered 1,325. The secular institutions then entered, which is to say, the officers of the high court, the medical tribunal, the merchant guild or *consulado*, the university rector, doctors and masters and the city council. They were followed by the public display of the royal insignia, the sceptre, mace and imperial crown, escorted by the knights of the military orders, and followed by the Crown's fiscal officers, in customs, treasury and the court of audit, and then by the *audiencia*, the high court of justice. Finally there came the viceroy, the Marquis of Mancera, escorted by three companies of infantry, each numbering a hundred men. As will be observed, on these ceremonial occasions, virtually no one walked as an individual citizen or subject; participation depended on membership of an institution or community. Similar, if less complete, processions sallied forth on the streets of the capital during Holy Week, the feast of Corpus Christi and certain other occasions.

The arrival of a viceroy from Spain was always greeted by ceremonial entrance into the capital, during which he was expected to ride under wooden arches specially constructed by the city council and the cathedral chapter. The entrance of the Marquis of La Laguna in 1680 was notable because the chapter commissioned Sor Juana Inés de la Cruz, the leading poet of her age, to design their arch and set forth its meaning in her *Neptuno Alegórico*. For its part, the city council chose Carlos de Sigüenza y Góngora, a Creole patriot and polymath, to design their arch, and publish his commentary, *Teatro de virtudes políticas*. The latter construction was a grandiose affair, 90 feet high and 50 feet wide, and divided into three levels, supported by Corinthian pillars. It had sixteen niched pedestals reserved for emblematic statues. But whereas, on these occasions, the statues, inscriptions and commentaries usually invoked classical figures and allusions, by contrast Sigüenza y Góngora reminded the viceroy that he had come to rule a city which had possessed a line of Indian monarchs prior to the Spanish conquest. The arch carried statues of twelve Mexican rulers and leaders, each taken to embody different political virtues. Whereas Huitzilihuitl was praised as a law-giver, the emperor Moctezuma Ilhuicamin was depicted as both a warrior and a protector of religion. In this pantheon, Cuauhtémoc figured as a native Cato, ever constant in adversity. The entire symbolic structure expressed the hope that on some future occasion the Mexican monarchs, whose heroic and imperial virtues offered lessons in statecraft as inspiring as any ancient Roman or Greek, 'might be reborn from the ashes to which oblivion has consigned them, so that, like western phoenixes, they may be immortalized by fame . . '.[5]

It fell to Sigüenza y Góngora to describe the disastrous events of 1692, when the maize crop failed, owing to an infection; prices rose to unparalleled heights; and the populace rioted. Neither the efforts of the religious who sallied forth carrying the sacrament, nor of the viceregal guard could restrain the mob, which looted the textile stalls of the great import merchants and then invaded the viceregal palace and set fire to part of the building. As a scholar, Sigüenza y Góngora went out to rescue the city archive from destruction and condemned the populace as 'a common people so very common' that was composed of Indians, of Blacks both from Africa and the locally born, of a whole range of mixed races, and of 'Spaniards who are the worst among such a vile mob'.[6] In particular, he denounced the Indians whom he described as entirely given over to drunkenness and who hated 'we Spaniards'. He asserted that by then more *pulque*, an alcoholic drink made from the fermented juice of the maguey, was drunk in a single day than in an entire year before the Conquest. In effect, this Creole patriot did not entertain any concept of a Mexican nation that might comprise all the different ethnic groups into which the population was then divided. He was the spokesman of a class rather than of a nation.

Virtually all the clerical contemporaries of Sigüenza y Góngora complained of the drunkenness of all classes of Indian society, defining it as the cause of constant quarrels, infidelities and even murder. The Italian traveller Giovanni Francesco Gemelli Careri, who visited New Spain in the 1690s, was appalled by the populace of the capital, characterizing the Blacks as insolent and threatening and the Indians as indolent and downtrodden, the two groups united only by a common addiction to theft and drink. So also, he commented that the great import merchants were mainly immigrants from Spain, whose Creole sons often quarrelled bitterly with their fathers, whereas Creole women 'have a great affection for Europeans . . . whom though poor, they prefer to marry rather than their compatriots',[7] since the latter consorted with Mulatto women. Much the same comments were advanced by Francisco de Ajofrín, a Spanish Capuchin who visited Mexico in 1763. He exclaimed that the number of poor in Mexico and Puebla far exceeded anything he had seen in Spain, since 'of a hundred persons you might meet on the streets, you will hardly find one who is properly dressed

[5] Carlos de Sigüenza y Góngora, *Seis obras*, ed. William G. Bryant (Caracas: Biblioteca Ayacucho, 1984), pp. 167–8.

[6] *Ibid.*, pp. 113–14, 123.

[7] Gemelli Careri and Giovanni Francesco, *Viaje a la Nueva España* ed. Francisca Perujo (Mexico: Universidad Nacional Autónoma de México, 1976), p. 22.

and shod'. He found it painful to observe the sharp contrast between the mansions and fine carriages of the rich and the hovels and rags of the poor, and concluded: 'In this city can be seen two extremes sharply opposed: much wealth and the greatest poverty; many fine clothes and the greatest nakedness; great cleanliness and much filth.'[8] Similarly, he commented that Creoles did not display much business sense and often dissipated the fortunes they inherited from their immigrant parents.

The accession of the Bourbon dynasty to the Spanish throne in 1700 had little immediate effect on Mexico. Indeed, from the 1640s until the 1760s, New Spain developed according to its own rhythm without any obvious metropolitan intervention. Native-born Spaniards came to dominate both the cathedral chapters and the city councils, and after the 1680s, when the purchase of office was introduced, the *audiencias* were also dominated by Creoles. Much the same was true of the religious orders and the parochial clergy. It was in this extended century that the bulk of the churches and convents in Mexico City were built or reinforced and decorated. In 1648, when Spain was torn by civil war and rebellion, the city of Puebla, led by the controversial bishop Juan de Palafox y Mendoza, celebrated the consecration of its cathedral. Then, in 1667, the city of Mexico followed suit, when members of its leading institutions entered the great cathedral for its consecration and listened to the sermon pronounced by Isidro Sariñana, who reminded them that work had begun in 1573 and that the building of a edifice that measured 393 feet long and 192 feet wide had cost some 1,752,000 pesos.

From the 1720s until the 1780s, the Mexican Church, led by the cathedral chapter of the capital, not to mention the Society of Jesus, sponsored the adoption of the churrigueresque style of decoration. In 1727 the exuberant 'Altar de los Reyes', constructed in the apse of the cathedral, was completed by Jerónimo de Balbás, who in 1709 had designed a similar altar-piece or *retablo* for the *sagrario* or cathedral parish church in Seville. Such was its impact that other churches began to install altar-pieces in this style. In 1747 Lorenzo Ramírez, another Spanish architect, completed the *sagrario* of the cathedral covering its facades with *estípetes*, the key device of the churrigueresque, an elaborate Spanish baroque style of sculptural and architectural ornament, in which pillars were broken down into geometric contours and loaded with niched pedestals for statues. Here was a style, already present in Andalucia, which was greatly extended in New Spain

[8] Francisco de Ajofrín, *Diario del viaje que por orden de la Sagrada Congregación de Propaganda Fide hizo a la América Septentrional en el siglo XVIII el p[adre] fray Francisco de Ajofrín*, vol. 1, ed. Vicente Castañeda y Alcover (Madrid: Real Academia de la Historia, 1958–1959), p. 80.

and not extinguished until the 1780s. It was in the 1740s that the Jesuits completed the construction of the great College of San Ildefonso.

In 1736 the peaceful development of the capital was interrupted by the irruption of a savage epidemic of 'matlazahuatl', a plague usually identified as typhus or typhoid fever, which first appeared in the textile workshops, only then in 1737 to afflict the entire city. By January the sepulchres of the cathedral and the parish churches were overflowing, so that their air was filled with 'an intolerable stench'. At the cemetery of San Lázaro, hitherto reserved for lepers, the corpses of the poor were burnt, the daily pyre polluting the atmosphere for several months. In his *Escudo de armas de México* (1746), Cayetano de Cabrera y Oquendo, a Creole poet and playwright, compiled an extraordinary description of a city under siege (Figure 3.1). He noted that Juan Antonio de Vizarrón y Eguiarreta, archbishop of Mexico from 1730 to 1747 and viceroy of New Spain from 1734 to 1740, took the lead in distributing medicine and food and that his example was followed by many individual priests. In particular, the Jesuits, the Oratorians and the missionary Franciscans of San Fernando cared for the sick with exemplary devotion, at times sacrificing their own lives. For all that, by September, when the epidemic subsided, some 40,157 deaths had been recorded. Many of the poor, especially Indians, had died through abandonment, once their infection became obvious, and small children often suffered the fate of their parents.

With no system of quarantine and ineffectual cures, the city turned to spiritual remedies, which is to say, apart from prayers and masses, the clergy sponsored the parade through the streets of various much venerated holy images of the Virgin Mary and Christ, if without noticeable effect. It was at this point that both the city council and the cathedral chapter voted to proclaim Our Lady of Guadalupe as principal patron of the city. The Andalucian archbishop-viceroy accepted their proposal and on 27 April 1737 two councillors and two canons entered the palace to swear a solemn oath accepting the Virgin as the city's patron, later saluting her as 'Queen and Empress of Imperial Mexico, Most Holy Mary in her image of Guadalupe'. By then the cult of the Mexican Virgin had spread across New Spain, with the result that city councils and cathedral chapters, one by one, also swore to recognize her as patron. On 4 December 1746, the same two city councillors and the two canons (now dignitaries), entered the archbishop's bedroom, where he lay ill, and, acting as the authorized delegates of 'all the venerable ecclesiastical chapters and all the most noble cities and councils of this New Spain and those of Guatemala, New Galicia and Vizcaya' swore to take 'Our Lady the Virgin Mary in her prodigious advocation of Guadalupe' as their 'Universal and General Patron'. These proceedings were based on the premise that New Spain was a Christian

Figure 3.1 The 1736–7 epidemic of 'matlazahuatl.' Cayetano de Cabrera y Quintero, *Escudo de armas de México* (Mexico, 1746).

commonwealth, governed and led in equal measure by its temporal and spiritual authorities, endowed with the power and right to undertake these collective acts without prior reference to Madrid or Rome. For all that, when Benedict XVI approved of Mexico's choice of patron in a bull dated 25 May 1754, the capital celebrated with a triduum of masses and sermons, during which Francisco Javier Lazcano, a Jesuit theologian, praised the city as 'our imperial court, head of Septentrional America'. These celebrations marked the apogee of Creole patriotism.

The Seven Years' War (1756–63) and the accession of Charles III (1759–88) marked a watershed in the life of New Spain, since the Crown's imperial authority was reasserted and a new colonial state created. Once peace was declared, two regiments of Spanish infantry arrived, ostensibly to protect Mexico from British invasion, but equally to strengthen viceregal government. Then, José de Gálvez was sent to conduct a thorough-going visitation of the colony, from 1765 to 1771, during which he sought to enlarge the sources of royal revenue by creating the tobacco monopoly and placing the customs and excise service under direct administration. It was Gálvez and Francisco de Croix, the Flemish viceroy, who in 1767 implemented the royal command to expel all Jesuits from New Spain, and on encountering popular riots of protest crushed these movements with unparalleled severity. At one stroke the Creole elite were deprived of their most zealous and intelligent spiritual directors and teachers. The great College of San Ildefonso at this time had maintained 300 students, from whom there later emerged 'distinguished men, bishops, judges, canons and professors of all faculties'. Of the 678 members of the Mexican province, over 500 were Creoles, among them several of the highest talents of their generation, who were condemned to eke out the remainder of their lives in a penurious Italian exile. Moreover, when Gálvez became Minister of the Indies in 1776, he actively discriminated against the appointment of Creoles to high office, sending over to New Spain a host of young Spaniards to administer its government and revenue.

If the great object of Bourbon reforms was to increase trade and silver production in order to procure a greater fiscal profit for the Crown, Charles III and his ministers also favoured the neoclassical style in architecture and the arts, and in order to encourage its diffusion established in 1783 the Academy of San Carlos. Whereas the leading painter of Mexico in the 1750s was Miguel Cabrera, a native of Oaxaca, by contrast from the 1790s onwards the chief artist was Manuel Tolsá, a native of Valencia, who was skilled as much in architecture as in sculpture. His greatest achievement was the design and construction of the Palacio de Minería or Mining Palace (1797–1813), erected to house the newly created mining court, the administrative head of the mining guild. It also administered a mining college in the same building, which was the first secular institute of education in New Spain, since its pupils were expected to study metallurgy, chemistry, physics and mineralogy. The director of the college was Fausto de Elhuyar, a Basque who had studied at Freiburg. In all this, we may observe the degree to which Mexico, hitherto so secluded from European contact, was now exposed to new currents of thought and style.

The most formidable exponent of the enlightened despotism favoured by Charles III and his ministers was the Count of Revillagigedo, viceroy of New Spain (1789–94), who dedicated part of his administrative energy to the embellishment of the great square of Mexico City. According to a contemporary witness, the popular market that dominated a large part of the Zócalo was 'a confused labyrinth of huts made of matting and straw', from which were sold vegetables and fruits, poultry, dried meats, fish, pulque, bread and cooked foodstuff. Many of the owners of these stalls slept there at night, along with their dogs, the occasional cow, and the odd lover. The result of this social promiscuity was 'an intolerable stench'. Moreover, the great fountain, from which drinking water came, was also used to wash clothes. And when the rains fell, the whole area was covered with mud. As for the broad streets that approached the square, the *acequias*, the water trenches that ran down their centre, were open sewers that carried off domestic waste, but at times served as graves for the drunkards who fell into them. In effect, so this critic averred: 'for nearly three centuries Mexico has remained a filthy sink, a pestilent cesspit, a horrible sewer'.[9] It was Revillagigedo who removed the popular market, paved the square, covered over the main sewers and introduced lighting. His successor was to crown his achievement by placing the majestic equestrian statue of Charles IV, Tolsá's finest work, at the centre of the Zócalo.

The repaving of the square led to the discovery of the famous Mexica sculptures, the Piedra del Sol or Calendar Stone, and the goddess Coatlicue, which had been buried there after the conquest. Their discovery caused great excitement among the Creole elite and in 1792 Antonio de León y Gama published his *Descripción histórica y cronológica de las dos piedras*, whose censor declared that although European philosophers had sought to place 'the Indian nation at the level closest to that of beasts . . . this single feature of Indian culture will dispel all such gross errors'.[10] In effect, León y Gama's work marked the beginning of a rational archaeology in Mexico. But the patriotic significance of these discoveries was raised to another dimension

---

[9] *El segundo conde de Revillagigedo (Juicio de Residencia)*, Publicaciones del Archivo General de la Nacion, no. 22 (Mexico City, 1933), pp. 70, 326–8, 395, 451.
[10] Antonio de León y Gama, *Descripción histórica y cronológica de las dos piedras* (Mexico: Manuel Porrúa, 1978) unpaginated introduction.

by Fray Servando Teresa de Mier, a Dominican, who in a sermon delivered in the sanctuary of Our Lady of Guadalupe at Tepeyac on 12 December 1794 declared that the Piedra del Sol contained a hieroglyphic account of the mission of Saint Thomas the Apostle to ancient Anáhuac and that he had brought with him painted on his cape, the image of the Mexican Virgin. Condemned to immediate exile, Fray Servando was later to emerge as the historian and ideologue of the Mexican insurgency led by Miguel Hidalgo and José María Morelos.

When Alexander von Humboldt visited Mexico in 1803, he came with a recommendation from the Spanish Government and was enthusiastically welcomed by royal officials and the Creole elite. He was given virtually unrestricted access to official papers, ranging from the results of the 1792 census, to revenue accounts, and to recent geographical measurements of the northern territories. His *Essai politique sur le royaume de la Nouvelle-Espagne* (1807–11) was a vast compendium of information which drew upon his specialized knowledge of geology and mining, but which also summarized the collective endeavours of both the Bourbon bureaucracy and of Creole savants. In many ways, Humboldt was as much an editor as an author, the spokesman of the Bourbon administrative Enlightenment. All the emphasis was upon recent achievements and almost no mention was made of the cultural efflorescence of Mexico during the preceding epoch. To be sure, Humboldt admired the cathedral, but reserved his praise for Tolsa's equestrian statue and yet more for the Mining Palace, which he described as a building fit to grace the streets of Naples or Rome. By contrast, he was puzzled and repelled by the cathedral *sagrario*, which he deemed to have been built in a 'Moorish or Gothic' style. In his magisterial survey of Mexican mining, he used the information provided by Fausto de Elhuyar and the teachers of the mining college. Like all visitors to colonial Mexico, he commented on the ill-feeling that divided European and American Spaniards and noted the trend for Creoles to describe themselves simply as Americans. So too, he described New Spain as a country characterized by 'a monstrous inequality of rights and fortunes' and viewed the isolation and retardation of the Indian communities as the greatest obstacle to the country's progress. For all that, Humboldt painted a dazzling portrait of New Spain as a country of great wealth, of vast extension, and of untapped possibilities. At no point, however, did he perceive any demand for independence.

Further Reading

Brading, D. A., *The First America. The Spanish Monarchy, Creole Patriots, and the Liberal State* 1492–1867 (Cambridge: Cambridge University Press, 1991).

——, *Mexican Phoenix. Our Lady of Guadalupe: Image and Tradition across Five Centuries* (Cambridge: Cambridge University Press, 2001).

Kubler, George and Martin Soria, *Art and Architecture in Spain and Portugal and their American Dominions* 1500 to 1800 (Baltimore and London: Penguin Books, 1959).

Ramos Medina, Manuel (ed.), *Historia de la ciudad de México en los fines de siglo XV–XX* (Mexico: Grupo Carso, 2001).

Tovar de Teresa, Guillermo, *La ciudad de México y la utopía en el siglo XVI* (Mexico City: Espejo de Obsidiana Ediciones, 1987).

Von Humboldt, Alexander, *Political Essay on the Kingdom of New Spain*, trans. John Black, 4 vols (London: Longman and Co., 1811).

4. THE MODERN CITY
From the Reforma-Peralvillo to the Torre Bicentenario: the Clash of 'History' and 'Progress' in the Urban Development of Modern Mexico City
DIANE E. DAVIS

The invitation to reflect on modern Mexico City is a rather daunting challenge, for the subject remains elusive or, better said, open to debate and definition. After all, what exactly constitutes modern Mexico City? Or, stated differently, *when* does Mexico City become modern? Is there a clear distinction between historic and modern Mexico City, or to use the categories of the other chapters in this volume, between pre-Colombian, colonial and modern Mexico City? And does this distinction hold up throughout the twentieth century, when we see the mix of these legacies and their coexistence over time?

Just as complicated is the question of *what* exactly it is that makes Mexico City modern—not just with respect to the *longue dureé* of its chronological past, but also within the past century. Is it something tangible, perhaps even visible, that is evident in the city's built environment, that is, in its architecture and land use? Or, might it also be traced to politics and the economy, or even to the social and cultural life of the city? And even if we could answer these questions, what about the issue of variation over space and not just time? That is, should Mexico City's 'modernity' or history, or the unique mix of the two, be identifiable only in certain parts of the city, like for example its downtown or perhaps in the *chinampas* of Xochimilco, or all over?

Questions about how, where and in what identifiable ways past and present combine in modern Mexico City are essentially questions about the semiotics of history and modernity, which in turn lead to a third set of enquiries having to do with agency, or who—or what forces—are responsible for the predominance and/or mix of tradition and modernity in twentieth-century Mexico? Do certain actors and institutions claim the authority—or legitimacy—to make this determination, on what basis, with or without opposition or conflict, and with what impact on the city?

55

What history, whose culture?

These are difficult questions to answer, primarily because so much of the present beauty, appeal, and magic of Mexico City is still intricately embedded in the past, and vice versa—if not in political terms, where the demise of one-party rule has broken historical connections—then in cultural, identity, and built environmental terms, where there is considerable continuity with earlier decades and centuries. But much more important, these are critical and compelling questions because there are no clear answers to them, and, perhaps most significantly, because they have been struggled over for at least the last seventy years, if not longer, and are still being challenged.

Over the past year or so, conflict and controversy over building removal and renovation in Mexico City—in key areas of its historic centre and several locations in the metropolitan area—have brought questions of history and the city's future into the limelight. A recent project that propelled such concerns was the Torre Bicentenario (Bicentennial Tower), a proposed skyscraper project designed by the eminently modernist Dutch architect Rem Koolhaas, initially supported by Mexico City Mayor Marcelo Ebrard as part of a plan to catapult Mexico City into the ranks of world cities along the lines of London, and setting Mexico City ahead of the pack of Latin American cities in reaching a new state of modernity. Its specifications describe it as being Latin America's tallest building, at a proposed height of 300 metres; they also highlight its sustainable character and 'intelligent infrastructure', to use the lingo of green, architectural and planning professionals (Figure 4.1).

Equally important, this building was intended to honour national history not only in its nomenclature, but also with its projected opening date of 2010, in commemoration of the 200th anniversary of Mexican independence from colonial rule. Since his election in July 2007 on the banner of the Partido de la Revolución Democrática (or PRD), Mayor Marcelo Ebrard and his principal urban advisor, Dr Alejandra Moreno Toscano, have planned a set of projects and activities to celebrate the bicentennial. Dr Moreno Toscano, a leading historian of Mexico City with impeccable academic credentials who now serves as the main policy authority for the historic centre, is committed to keeping historical continuities alive as the city uses a celebration of the past to lead it into the future. The proposed Torre Bicentenario, although offered by private developers and not city officials themselves, was conceived as just such a hybrid of past and future, tradition and modernity, all wrapped up in one highly visible package. It also was conceived as complementary to larger urban planning objectives. Both Mayor Ebrard and Moreno Toscano have been committed to bringing much needed investments into the urban renovation of Mexico City, in

Figure 4.1 Design of the proposed Torre Bicentenario, Mexico City. © Office for Metropolitan Architecture.

order to make the city a global capital worthy of future investments. And while a main concern had been to jump-start investments in more central areas of the Federal District where densities remained low, and to use property projects and urban policy measures to repopulate downtown and other areas of the city that had been losing population, this administration did initially support the Torre project.

But trouble lay ahead. As discursively skilful as the propaganda for the Torre appeared, with its semiotic references to both past and the future, and as important as the project may have been for the urban development aims of the current mayor and for his desire to use the 2010 bicentennial as a focal point for celebrating a renovated and forward-looking metropolis, it nonetheless met extraordinary resistance. Vocal opposition and heightened controversy surrounding the Torre played out daily in the press starting almost immediately, accelerating through the latter half of August and into September, until the project stalled and was eventually withdrawn in

October 2007. What had started as a potential public relations coup rapidly turned into a highly partisan political struggle in which citizens and elected local officials in the neighbourhood designated to host the new project vehemently opposed the plan. The leading voices of opposition were not merely citizens with a commitment to grassroots urban planning, however, but high level personnel connected to the Partido de Acción Nacional (PAN), the centre-right political party now governing the Federal Executive.

The PAN has engaged in both front and backstage battle with the PRD leadership in Mexico City since the July 2006 elections, when the previous PRD mayor, Andres Manuel López Obrador, lost the electoral count by a fraction and declared himself the 'legitimate president' of Mexico. But it wasn't merely PANista-generated citizen opposition that killed this project. A key protagonist in the battle was the National Institute of Fine Arts (Instituto Nacional de Bellas Artes, or INBA), a federal agency granted the legal authority to protect Mexico's post-nineteenth century historic and cultural patrimony.

As soon as the project was announced, INBA administrators raised historic and cultural objections about its appropriateness, primarily because the plan called for the destruction of the Súper Servicio Lomas, a building on the site of the proposed project (see Figure 4.2). Built in 1948 by Russian émigré architect Vladimir Kaspé, the Súper Servicio Lomas enjoyed architectural status as one of the first 'multi-use buildings in Mexico'. And although it has been neglected for years, housing a petrol station, a car dealership, shops and a restaurant, the Instituto de Investigaciones Estéticas of the National University has called it a fundamental work of the Modern Movement in Mexican architecture. Based on such attributions, in August the INBA declared the Súper Servicio Lomas to be key element of the nation's historic and cultural patrimony and 'provisionally' halted the Torre Bicentenario project, which, as noted above, in late October was dropped completely.

Outside observers are in no position to comment on the character or accuracy of the INBA's or the Instituto de Investigaciones Estéticas's assessments of the cultural or historical value of the original building. But the ironies of the decision do require some comment. A twenty-first-century modernist skyscraper was jettisoned because the nation's designated history and culture authorities sought to save a mid-twentieth-century modernist project from destruction. This building was less than sixty years old. That it was conceived and designed by a foreign architect, moreover, seems not to have mattered to the INBA, despite its charge to conserve national patrimony—although this does raise further questions about the role of INBA as a national institution to preserve *Mexican* culture. Even if we

Figure 4.2 Vacant workshops of Súper Servicio Lomas. Photograph by Gareth Jones.

acknowledge the hybridity of the notion of 'Mexican-ness' in a country that suffered through colonial as well as imperial conquest, the question of what is foreign and what is indigenous is both compelling and complex, and thus worthy of some reflection. Should the procedures used to recognize or protect colonial monuments and buildings be the same as those applying to indigenous residues of the pre-Colombian past, and should either or both travel without modification to the twentieth century? In some ways the latter is an epistemological question about dividing lines— in terms of historical or cultural patrimony—within 'modernity' as much as it is about technical expertise. Does a sixty-year-old modernist project truly have more historical or cultural value than a brand new modernist project, especially if one's vantage point is the future?

Such queries also raise questions about the rationale for protecting the past versus the future of Mexico City, and about the role of the built environment and historic preservation as juxtaposed against other measures for achieving urban developmental aims. Does the Súper Servicio Lomas, which celebrates the car culture that helped produce the sprawl and environmental degradation of the city, matter more than the new modernist project that is intended to remedy these problems by densifying and refocusing urban land use?

The paradoxes surrounding the controversy over the Torre Bicentenario and the protection of the Súper Servicio Lomas are such that one must wonder whether the controversy was less about history and culture per se, and whether other issues were involved. Among them, two possibilities stand out: partisan political conflict between Mayor Ebrard and his political opponents, and the uneasy and still ambiguous fault lines between city officials (Distrito Federal) and federal authorities. Both sets of tensions have accelerated in recent years, owing to the recent democratization of the political system. Yet even if recent patterns of democratization and liberalization lurk behind this particular controversy over historic preservation, such battles and struggles are nothing new. Questions about who has the right to destroy old buildings and neighbourhoods, and for what purpose, have marked urban policy discussions in Mexico City for decades, with some of the first and most virulent of these conflicts revolving around the efforts to widen a key downtown thoroughfare, Avenida Reforma-Peralvillo, during the early 1950s.

What has changed, however, are the players, the political and economic stakes involved, and, most importantly, the role of cultural and historical authorities like the INBA and its sister institution the INAH (Instituto Nacional de Arqueología e Historia), in mediating these conflicts and determining the fate of the built environment. Preliminary evidence from the Torre controversy and other recent projects suggests that the INAH and INBA are acting much more imposingly than in the past, hence leading to outcomes such as the stalled project mentioned above.

This chapter aims to give a brief historical account of why this is the case, focusing on pressures to preserve Mexico City's past (i.e. its history and culture), the ways they have been juxtaposed against plans for its future, and how the balance of these views has shifted over time. It identifies the key actors and institutions who have embraced 'history' as opposed to 'progress', determines which set of forces have predominated at which moments in the city's twentieth-century history, and assesses the long-term implications of the shifting balance for the social, spatial and built environmental character of the city. The chapter concludes with discussion of the current role that cultural and historical authorities now play in determining the fate of the city, raising questions about the implications of this shift for urban planning and urban life in contemporary Mexico City.

Urbanization-led industrialization and a new face for the city, 1950–65

Conflicts between forces that sought to preserve rather than destroy the city's built environmental history date to the late 1940s and early 1950s, at a time when Mexico's leaders were eager to bring sustainable prosperity to both the capital and the nation. In this period, alliances were made between political leaders, the economic elite and the working class to foment a national industrialization project, much of it physically centred on Mexico City. During the Presidency of Miguel Aleman (1946–52), the capital's reputation as a location for both industrial and commercial development reached new heights. In response, governing officials sought a massive new transportation grid that would allow greater mobility of labourers commuting to the industrial peripheries of the city while also increasing access to commercial establishments downtown.

The new transportation plan depended on an August 1950 proposal to widen one of the city's oldest boulevards, the Avenida Reforma, and extend it to an area in the city called Peralvillo. This project, called the Reforma–Peralvillo extension, was articulated in terms of transport efficiency and infrastructural support for the creation of a prosperous zone for central city commerce. It entailed extensive urban renewal plans built around a commitment to expanding key streets in and around the historic centre, building new pavements for pedestrian usage and constructing new parking areas. Yet each of these objectives called for some destruction of the built environment, mainly the colonial and pre-colonial buildings that peppered the city centre, which had long been a work and residential mecca for seasonal and permanent rural migrants journeying downtown to buy and sell in the historic market culture that had defined Mexico City since Aztec times.

Promoters of built environmental changes embodied in this project included the local chamber of commerce and middle-class property owners who sought to eliminate street traders and other 'uncivilized' rural migrants or low income residents, in part because their street vending activities limited vehicle access and because their continued residential presence (sustained by rent control) put a cap on property development. The concerns of those seeking to 'modernize' the city's transport infrastructure were given a platform in the city's Planning Commission, whose members were named by the presidentially appointed mayor and who came from the private sector (industry, commerce, and banking), several government agencies (pubic works, public health, communications, treasury), and professional associations of engineers and architects working for the city government.

In this initial period, most conflict remained behind the scenes, mainly because no representatives from the institutional 'keepers of history' (INAH and INBA) sat on the Planning Commission, thereby allowing most of the first years of city planning to be undertaken without serious rebuke from historic preservationists. Still, objections were raised to street widening by residents who were to be dislodged by the project, which called for a destruction of almost 300 properties or 500 buildings and the displacement of an estimated 25,000 individuals. Moreover, as soon as the proposed project became known, representatives from INAH publicly decried the destructive consequences of these urban modernization plans. They called for protection of the physical and cultural heritage of the city from the so-called modernizers who sought to turn it into a 'prototypical US metropolis', characterized by wide vehicle-friendly streets with no visible remnants of street commerce.

Given the limited political power of the city's low income residents and small-scale commercial actors (primarily street vendors or small retailers), and the fact that INAH and INBA had no voice on the Planning Commission, the street-widening project remained alive despite criticism. Many of its key elements were approved and implemented—acts which INAH officials later characterized as the 'ruthless destruction' of several key colonial monuments in historic centre, undertaken in a fit of 'technical barbarism'. Even so, the city's modernizers were not fully triumphant. Sustained public outcry over the initial implementation of the plan, and the fact that even in the Planning Commission the project squeaked through with a vote of 8:6 in support, ensured that the voices of 'progress' remained under challenge even after the initial construction began. INAH, and especially its inspectors in the Division on Colonial Monuments, continued its protest against the destruction of several noteworthy seventeenth- and eighteenth-century convents and colonial monuments, and by so doing brought larger swathes of the public to their side.

Protests soon widened to include a long list of intellectuals and artists, including Diego Rivera, Frida Kahlo and scores of leading historians and anthropologists. Joining them in decrying the destructive urban changes were the city's small-scale commercial producers, who formed a strong political base for the incoming mayor, Ernesto Uruchurtu (1952–65). When representatives from INAH were subsequently invited to join the Planning Commission, the balance of support shifted away from the modernizers, establishing a new phase in the battle between the forces of history and progress, with Mayor Uruchurtu playing the mediator.

With Uruchurtu at the helm a new set of urban priorities emerged, straddling the concerns of both history and progress. Support for prosperity still dominated the agenda, but tempered with a commitment to preserving middle-class culture broadly defined. In particular, he sought to preserve the cultures *and* the buildings of downtown, not to mention local economic bases for prosperity, in a way that focused attention on the middle income groups that had fallen between the cracks of prior visions.

Over the 1950s Uruchurtu greatly reduced the ambitious programme of street widening advanced by his predecessors, limiting it to a few key streets where displacement would be minimal. He also halted several related urban renewal projects that threatened to destroy the commercial character and historic markets of the area, including a proposed plan to raze and replace the iconic La Lagunilla market with a modern shopping mall. Instead, he focused on improving the existing buildings, services and infrastructure. In addition to recognizing the cultural value and importance of downtown commercial life for retail consumers and producers, Uruchurtu funded the beautification of downtown parks by investing in flowers, green spaces and fountains; he imposed strict regulations on nightclubs, social clubs and prostitution, so that downtown could remain a place for families to stroll, shop and interact; and he prioritized the development of drainage infrastructure to reduce flooding and water-borne disease that made city-centre streets impassable during the rainy season.

In compensation for any destruction that would result from his infrastructure or beautification programmes, Uruchurtu also initiated a programme of housing construction for middle-class residents—many of them government employees who lived downtown and worked in government offices in the central city. He took special care to ensure that the new residential complexes would not completely displace downtown residents, but rather, relocate them to safer and more open areas still in walking distance of the historic city centre. This allowed a renovation of sorts, but without full expulsion of middle-class residents. Perhaps the most important project of this kind was the Tlatelolco-Nonoalco Housing Estate, built for government employees in 1964 and described by its developers as a project intended to 'restore *el Centro*, remove its inhabitants, and convert the area into an eminently cultural and touristic zone by reserving the use of buildings and monuments for primarily institutional functions'.[1]

With this more integrated effort to accommodate the city's history *and* improve the downtown built environment without sacrificing buildings for people, or vice versa, Uruchurtu forged a new path, different from that proposed by the advocates of history or progress in the 1940s. Even so, he inadvertently kept the nascent tensions between these divergent views of history and progress alive by creating institutional linkages and dialogue

---

[1] Hector Manuel Romero, *Historia del transporte en la Ciudad de México: De la trajinera al metro* (Mexico City: Secretaría General de Desarrollo Social, 1987), p. 35.

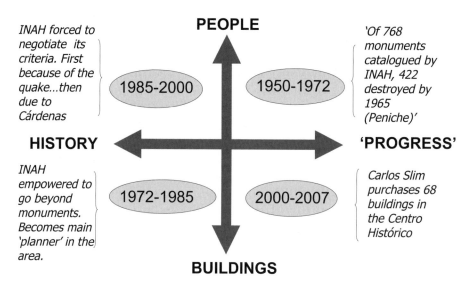

Figure 4.3 Conjunctures of preservation and progress, 1950–2007.

with both preservationists in the INAH and private sector developers or other urban modernizers. With all these voices incorporated in the Planning Commission and into the programmes of his administration more generally, no single view could completely dominate urban plans. This made it easier for Uruchurtu to put his own spin on the discussion, defining both 'history' and 'progress' through the lens of middle-class preferences. The result was a unique hybrid of objectives in which the historic centre remained a haven for middle classes, both privileged and poor, and in which historic buildings and longstanding cultural traditions remained relatively intact.

Steadying the precarious balance, 1965–85

Much of Uruchurtu's popularity was the result of his concerted efforts to reign in both high-end property developers and low-end retailers and street vendors in the historic centre. He accomplished this through heavy-handed police efforts to rid the city of street vendors, but without destroying the streets or historic buildings they used as a base, and through stubborn opposition to the construction of a subway in downtown Mexico City, a project strongly supported by the city's main property developers and one of the country's largest construction firms. Yet ultimately, these unpopular stances created political problems for Uruchurtu, primarily because they challenged the forces who were gaining in number if not influence by the end of his term, both street vendors and property developers.

With changes in the macro-economy signalling a nascent decline in the import-substitution industrialization model, the ranks of informal sellers began to swell as fewer industrial jobs were created. At the same time, decreasing competitiveness of industry drove ever more capitalists to look for property development as a key source of income generation. Uruchurtu, with his middle-class constituency, faced pressure from both these forces as well as from residents and developers who decried the congested street conditions and/or wasted property development potential downtown. In 1967 party leaders responded by pressuring Uruchurtu to resign. Perhaps the last straw was his intransigence over a proposed subway project for downtown, promoted by major urban developers, construction interests and Mexico's President as a means of transforming downtown land use, and thus land values, without calling for massive levelling of buildings or widening of streets. To some, this project seemed the perfect solution for both protecting downtown history and promoting urban and economic progress. But the subway and the vision of the city it projected also challenged many of the social and political relationships that Uruchurtu had forged, first with middle-class residents who feared displacement with property valuation and the destruction of traditional middle-class culture downtown, and second with the bus industry, who saw the subway as direct competition.

In the end, the very political relationships and cultural values that helped inform Uruchurtu's hybrid vision of history and progress, focused on protection of traditional middle-class culture and commerce downtown, also led to his forced resignation and the approval of the subway project. And with Uruchurtu gone, it appeared that the modernizers would again have the upper hand, giving them the power to once again define progress in terms of densifying downtown land use and growing the urban economy through commercial and property development, as in the late 1940s and early 1950s.

But even as ground was broken on the subway lines in 1967, a series of unexpected events shifted the balance back towards the voices of history sufficiently so as to keep a stalemate alive. In particular, excavation for new subway lines revealed significant archaeological sites underneath the surface of the historic Zócalo. This discovery brought pressures to privilege INAH and the voices of historic preservation in city planning decisions about housing, roads and other key infrastructure—changes that were mandated by new legislation like the Programa de Remodelación Urbana (1971–6) and the Ley Federal Sobre Monumentos y Zonas Arqueológicas, Artísticos, e Históricos (1972). As the ongoing excavation of city streets produced more treasures, including the discovery of the monumental sculpture of Coyolxahuqui by workers for the Companía de Luz y Fuerza (in turn leading to the discovery of the Templo Mayor), additional legislation formalized INAH's involvement. Perhaps the most significant was a law in 1980 declaring the Zócalo and its surrounds as a 'Historic Monument Zone'. That UNESCO developed and signed the convention for the Protection of World Cultural and Natural Heritage in 1972 may have raised consciousness about cultural and historical patrimony, but the initiative for these laws came from INAH, the government, and a few tourist-related industries seizing on the archaeological discoveries downtown as a way to renovate or promote the historic centre as a draw for visitors, both domestic and international (see Figure 4.4 for an elaboration of this timeline).

With INAH now holding legal power to halt urban projects that might harm historic sites downtown, the tables were turned and modernizers faced limits in their capacities to transform the city. The power of preservationist forces became manifest in the composition of the Consejo del

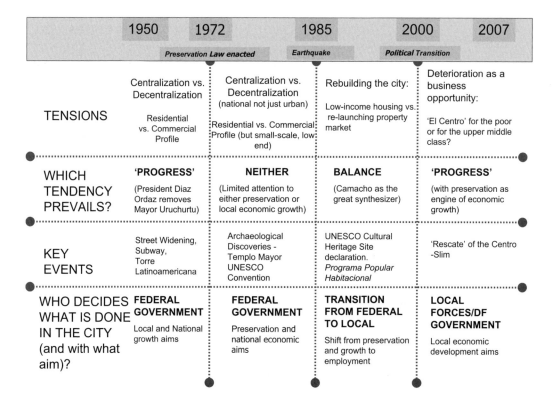

Figure 4.4 Tensions surrounding preservation and progress, 1950–2007.

Centro Histórico de la Ciudad de México, created in 1980, whose charge was 'to promote and coordinate public and private activities devoted to safeguarding the archaeological patrimony' of downtown. Council representatives included several federal secretariats (Public Education, Housing and Human Settlements, Public Works) as well as the Mexico City Mayor, the Rector of the National University, and the Director of INAH.

With private sector forces institutionally absent in this new body, few new construction or renewal projects materialized, meaning that land use, investment, and the commercial activities of the historic centre remained relatively stagnant. Downtown areas remained a shopping mecca for consumers, maintaining their mixed but relatively low rent land use and ensuring that the same middle- and lower middle-class government workers, retail employees and street vendors lived and worked downtown. The persistence of these more humble classes served as further disincentive for modernizers to seek new development projects, whether targeted towards the preservation or renewal of decayed buildings, or in terms of new buildings or activities. As a result, although protectionist voices prevailed, conditions deteriorated.

Two trends further accelerated the squalor of downtown spaces: 1) the steady outmigration of those middle classes who could afford to relocate to new subdivisions in the suburban periphery, leaving the poorer populations in the centre, and 2) the proliferation of new shopping malls in the suburban edge (e.g. Ciudad Satélite, Perisur), both of which curtailed demand for retail activities downtown. By the mid-1980s, with the downtown service economy and property market relatively stagnant, the situation alarmed both preservationists *and* modernizers. Governing officials responded in 1984 by creating a new executive arm of the Consejo, called the Vocalía Ejecutiva del Centro Histórico, to help coordinate and boost planning efforts for key historic sections of downtown.

Re-calibrating the balance of history and progress, 1985–2000

Before this new body could make headway on mixing preservationist and modernizing aims, a massive earthquake hit Mexico City in October 1985. The earthquake not only destroyed major portions of the historic centre, but also unsettled the established institutional, political, and economic relations among the divergent forces seeking to preserve or transform downtown, bringing property development advocates into the picture and jumpstarting new programmatic efforts to bring modernizing investors downtown (Figure 4.5).

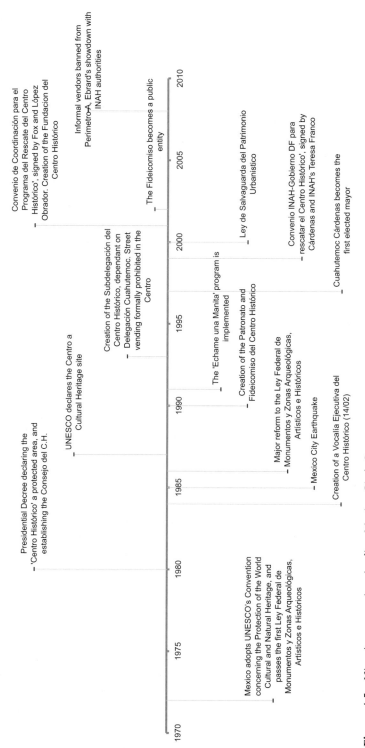

Figure 4.5 Historic preservation timeline, Mexico City's Centro

These changes were made possible because in 1985 the devastating earthquake damaged—and in some cases, levelled—many of the historic buildings in the downtown area, displacing thousands of residents and creating new demands for rebuilding. The most seriously affected held within their ranks low-income citizens who sought to remain downtown near sources of livelihood, many of whom joined together in collective claim-making for new urban policies to restore and revive downtown's economy and built environment. Most significantly, the displacement of citizens and destruction of buildings offered new opportunities for the clarification and/or re-establishment of downtown property rights, which in turn helped create both the supply and demand for downtown properties. All these changes brought renewed interest in downtown land parcels from property developers and, as a consequence, the creation of several new laws and governing bodies for managing or promoting reinvestment.

One was a petition to UNESCO in December 1986 to declare Mexico City's historic centre as 'patrimony for humanity', a request that was approved a year later. In October 1987 government officials joined with the historical and anthropological community to inaugurate the Museo del Templo Mayor, intended to display the archaeological riches downtown. Three years hence, in December 1990, public officials established a new coordinating agency for the area, called the Patronato del Centro Histórico, which operated with a separate executive financial arm for investments, called the Fideicomiso del Centro Histórico. While the Patronato accommodated a variety of spokespersons, including leading businessmen, its technical committee was dominated by public sector officials. And with both public and private sector officials involved in different aspects of its functioning, this new two-tiered body embodied a commitment to restoring monumental buildings and reviving a decaying downtown through the support of local residents as well as through new investments. It differed from many of its predecessor agencies, moreover, by focusing on questions of 'local economic development and protection of the local "social fabric"', a mandate large enough to include the housing and service concerns of local citizens as well as efforts to grow the local market through tourist-related restoration of museums, monuments and archaeological sites.

The Patronato del Centro Histórico partially revived the balanced vision of history and progress first established by Uruchurtu, but modified it to be more receptive to the idea of promoting downtown as a magnet for visitors seeking to partake of the area's rich cultural resources, and not solely for local residents. Over the 1990s, Mexico City hosted several new institutional initiatives and development programmes aimed towards deepening the commitment to downtown development goals. One introduced in 1991, called the 'Echame una Manita' programme,[2] gave fiscal incentives to anyone investing in the historic centre. The programme motivated forty property owners to sign letters of intent indicating a willingness to donate their abandoned or deteriorated properties to the Fideicomiso.

These institutional commitments produced few changes downtown, however, because the Mexico City government lacked sufficient resources to develop the parcels on its own. A further constraint was that when local public officials reached out to high profile investors to help finance property development and land use transformations, they often met organized popular opposition from local residents. With city officials facing struggles to democratize its governance apparatus throughout the first half of the 1990s (the president still appointed the mayor), local planners were particularly sensitive to citizen opposition to big development plans. Still, perhaps the biggest obstacle to private sector investment in sustained downtown development was the overall ambience of the area, particularly the enduring problems of street vending and informality.

After more than a decade of macro-economic crisis, Mexico City suffered growing unemployment and de-industrialization, trends that pushed ever more citizens into the informal sector. With small industrial workshops in the city closing in the face of global competition, and renewed investment in export-oriented industry in the northern parts of the country, residents found few employment alternatives, and informality and petty commerce continued to be the few available options other than emigration. These activities had long been a concern, but the 1990s saw an acceleration in the ranks of street vendors, and a renewed effort on the part of public officials to manage the problem. During his term, Mayor Manuel Camacho (1988–94) negotiated street vendor removal and relocation to newly built fixed commercial markets and, in the absence of significant gains, introduced a 1993 law prohibiting street vending in key downtown areas designated as historic patrimony.

These reforms failed to clear downtown streets, however, not just because street vendors remained a huge and powerful force to confront, but also because political conditions of the time were relatively unstable. Social movement opposition to PRI dominance had been percolating since the contested election of 1988, bringing a 1995 reform of the local electoral laws and paving the way for democratic election of Mexico City's mayor in 1997. In this transitional period, street vendors became important allies for the old politicians from the more centrist PRI, which sought to maintain political power and visibility in the capital, and for renegade political

---

[2] This programme name seemed particularly apt, translated both as 'lend me a helping hand' and 'give me a makeover'.

forces in the newly formed, left-leaning PRD. In a last-ditch effort to recover support from local residents, of which street vendors were a key constituency, PRI-affiliated Mayor Oscar Espinosa (1994–7) introduced a programme in 1996 called Vivir en el Centro, intended to shift the focus away from the high-end developments proposed by his predecessor and to cater to the local development concerns of local residents and small commerce.

Although this programme was cancelled when the 1997 mayoral election brought to office the PRD's Cuauhtémoc Cárdenas (1997–2000), the new mayor pursued a similar strategy with an added focus on popular housing, shunning upscale renovation and instead addressing the social and economic conditions of the city's lower- and middle-class residents, many of whom had supported the PRD in its electoral victory. His 1999 Plan Estratégico para la Regeneración y Desarrollo Integral del Centro Histórico de la Ciudad de México established the basic contours of this new approach, but focused on three key areas: the Alameda, the Centro Histórico and La Merced. All three areas depended on commercial activities as a main source of employment and economic growth, but they varied in their built environmental character.

A key concern for Cárdenas was the lack of adequate housing for local residents, and not merely the strengthening of low and high-end commerce, and both priorities came with a financial commitment from local government to try to achieve these goals. These aims brought the INAH back into the picture again. In July 1999 the Mexico City government signed a *convenio* (agreement) with INAH, producing what one ex-public official called 'splendid' relations between the city and historic preservation forces for the purposes of recovering 'the history and preserving the architectural patrimony of downtown while also addressing social and economic priorities of the residents'. To ensure this synthesis of aims, the two parties also formalized the creation of a *mesa de trabajo* (working group) to approve or deny requests for specific building projects and land-use plans that might affect downtown areas.

At this point, the 1972 and 1980 federal laws of historic preservation had formally granted authority to INAH to determine the fate of historic buildings, but since then the Institute had not been actively involved due to inadequate resources and the fact that most projects advanced during prior mayoral administrations were for new buildings on vacant downtown properties rather than renovations. Because Cárdenas's new vision built on a commitment to residential as well as commercial renewal, it required renovations or changes to facades and existent infrastructure, which meant that legally speaking INAH had to be involved. Accordingly, this period ushered in a new stage of cooperation between INAH and city officials, as well as renewed efforts to advance both history and progress, with the latter defined socially as well as economically.

Modernizing Mexico City and the new fault lines of conflict, 2000–7

The relatively cordial working relations between INAH and Mexico City officials did not last long, however, due to another set of political and legislative shifts unfolding barely a year later. In April 2000 the local legislature (Asamblea Legislativa del Distrito Federal, or ALDF) passed the Ley de Salvaguarda del Patrimonio Urbanistico Arquitectónico del Distrito Federal, whose Article 29 'establish[ed] general lines of public policy for safeguarding (the city's) urban architectural patrimony'. This new law allowed only a nominal role for the federal government through INAH and INBA, instead reinforcing the power of local authorities to force compliance with protective regulations, and giving the ALDF a direct role in authorizing permission for planned changes to buildings or public spaces protected under historic patrimony laws. Perhaps because this law sought to introduce yet another bureaucratic layer in an already complicated hierarchy of authorities, it did not produce immediate changes in urban decision-making. One ex-official of the Fideicomiso actually identified this law as relatively worthless, calling it a '*bodrio*' (literally a hodgepodge) that 'no one used or considered' because it was the result of partisan political negotiation in the ALDF.

Even if it was ignored by the Fideicomiso and other officials, the Ley de Salvaguarda did contribute to further confusion and a new round of disputes over which authorities had the final say over the built environmental history of downtown Mexico City. Things got dramatically worse when Manuel López Obrador (2000–4) became mayor. His ascent to office was accompanied by the resignation of the director of INAH in December 2000, after an eight-year career spanning mayoral administrations with both the PRI and PRD. A few months later, in August 2001, the mayor announced a massive downtown redevelopment plan focused on the 'rescue' of the historic centre.

Formally titled the Convenio de Coordinación para el Programa del Rescate del Centro Histórico, this August 2001 initiative counted on financial and political support from the nation's richest man, Carlos Slim, who allied with other important property investors and local businessmen to support the project. The plan also drew public support from Mexican President Vicente Fox of the centre-right Partido de Acción Nacional (PAN), whose signature on the *convenio* signalled a potential alliance between his administration, pro-private sector forces and Mayor López

Obrador around the issue of downtown property redevelopment. INAH's role, in contrast, was hardly visible, perhaps because the property redevelopment aims of the *convenio* were so defining. Whatever the reason, the heavy involvement of the private sector in the rescue plan became clear when López Obrador established a new coordinating body for making decisions, called the Fundación del Centro Histórico, and immediately named Carlos Slim as the president of its executive committee.

With most of the pro-property development ideas (and financing for them) emanating from the Fundación del Centro Histórico, in 2002 the longstanding Fideicomiso del Centro Histórico's status was converted from a private to a public entity, meaning that it no longer had access to private sector funds for the realization of its aims. Thus, even though the Fideicomiso remained a main coordinating body for mediating requests and permissions for property development in the historic centre, after 2002 this body coexisted—and competed—with the Fundación del Centro Histórico, which had a higher public profile, immense resources and relatively bold new urban development plans that diverged from past priorities, especially those of INAH. This combination of institutional fragmentation and overlap reduced the institutional capacity of INAH to oversee urban development objectives, with its power to protect historic buildings further diminished by Slim's marginalization of INAH forces within the deliberations led by the Fundación's executive committee. The result was growing tension between INAH and the coalition of local authorities and private sector developers, who were strongly supporting the rescue.

Just as important, these organizational changes and bureaucratic tensions had their impact on the history–progress balance, shifting the decision-making power away from the protagonists of history and towards those preoccupied with economic progress and prosperity. This is not to say that the Fundación ignored history or preservation as it sought to renew downtown; nor is it to say that INAH and other public sector representatives were entirely banished from decision-making over downtown property development. But INAH's role was greatly reduced from 2000, and its *de facto* power highly circumscribed, because the Fundación's priority was to reconstruct areas of the city where the most high-end consumer revenues could be extracted, whether through tourism or commerce. This objective meant that many historic buildings and sites of interest to INAH were completely off the Fundación's radar screen, and that spurring the urban economy through property development and commercialization of cultural patrimony was as much the aim as historic preservation. Both stances created a nascent turf battle over whose priorities would lay the foundation for urban change, with INAH steadily marginalized in *de facto* if not *de jure* terms.

As Mayor López Obrador's administration found itself in a low-grade conflict with INAH officials over whose authority should prevail with respect to urban renovation, its political room for manoeuvre was further limited by opposition from street vendors who were discontent with being removed from areas designated for rescue. They also lamented losing direct channels of communication with the mayor's office, now that the chain of urban decision-making authority for the historic centre rested in the Fundación, where big developers shared decision-making power with public officials. Street vendor dissatisfaction soon became a political problem for the mayor because this highly organized and large constituency was known to be a strong base for the PRD. Street-vendor organizations were particularly salient in discussions of downtown development because their activities were embedded in the historic economic traditions and culture of central city neighbourhoods, thereby providing direct entry to a much larger constituency of downtown residents who also feared displacement from upscale development.

In the context of this shifting balance of power and rising political dissatisfaction from street vendors and INAH, Mayor Marcelo Ebrard arrived in office in 2006, armed with yet another set of urban plans. Ebrard began his term as mayor seeking to deepen and expand the transformation of downtown Mexico City started by López Obrador and Slim through the Fundación. But he also hoped to widen aims beyond the upscale, high-end biases the Fundación had embodied to include a concern with the economic livelihood of local residents, including small commerce and street vendors, as well as with the physical conditions under which they and other low-income residents were living and working—whether in terms of housing or public space.

Clearly, few of these priorities were entirely new, with several having been picked up by mayors in prior epochs. But in contrast to previous administrations, Ebrard sought to maximize a commitment to a multiple aims, without sacrificing one set of priorities for the other. That is, he sought to preserve history by supporting the longstanding economic activities, cultures and peoples of the historic centre, *and* to incentivize property and real estate transformation. Like his predecessors, Ebrard knew that to accomplish these aims would require a new coordinating body for downtown; but in contrast to prior attempts, he created a new agency that would coordinate *all* urban policymaking for the historic centre, not merely decisions linked to property development and investment.

Thus, a month after taking office, he created a new type of administrative entity, called the Autoridad del Centro Histórico, and placed under its administrative authority almost every possible policy domain that could affect downtown: transport, policing, museums, cultural activities, infrastructure, job creation and so on, all along side the conventional concerns with housing and property development. Headed by the eminent urban historian Alejandra Moreno Toscano, who had served on the Fundación del Centro Histórico and thus had good relations with Carlos Slim and other property developers, this new body had tremendous power, although because its legal status was (and remains) uncertain, it took several months of existence and public vetting in the press until the Autoridad was *de facto* recognized as the guiding authority for downtown development. The fact that its head had tremendous respect in a wide range of constituencies, owing to her long career in public service and past involvement in socially and environmentally conscious urban and policy development for the Federal District, helped make this possible.

Yet even with the clear administrative potential to integrate history and progress embodied in the persona of Moreno Toscano, as well as in the institutionalization of the Autoridad and its wide-ranging urban policy reach from 2007 onwards, Ebrard's administration also faced growing antagonism from INAH, especially its rank-and-file inspectors, who sought to protect if not extend their reach in the domain of historic preservation (Figure 4.6). Some of this stemmed from the fact that the previous administration had marginalized INAH, a stance felt as a stinging rebuke to a legally sanctioned federal agency that prided itself on protecting Mexican culture and whose personnel enjoyed great respect in the academic, cultural and historical worlds. It also stemmed from the fact that intra-organizational tensions added complexity, producing a harder line from INAH administrators than might have been pursued had their rank-and-file employees not insisted. The combined result was growing conflict between INAH and the Ebrard administration, first showing its head in 2007 and ultimately leading to the rather ludicrous controversy over the Torre Bicentenario in summer 2008.

That relations between the two deteriorated so dramatically in the course of a year owes not just to the fact that the Torre was a controversial project, nor to the fact that the Súper Servicio Lomas was so worthy of protection, but rather, to the inter-institutional tensions over who would have the authority to plan for the city, and with what balance of commitments to history and progress. This fight became so visceral because it came in the midst of a much larger battle over the role of INAH in urban decision-making. The main problem was that Ebrard and Moreno Toscano had ambitious plans to balance both history and progress in new ways, and this meant placing decisions about historic preservation in the context of much larger urban planning aims in which they would have the final authority over the physical built environment, not INAH.

Figure 4.6 Suspension of building works authorized by INAH, downtown Mexico City, October 2007. Photograph by Onesimo Flores Dewey.

The nature of these objectives and how they alienated INAH and other purists of historical preservation are clear with a closer look at one of Mayor Ebrard's main initiatives upon coming to office, a 2007 plan to remove street vendors from the Perimetro A of the historic centre. The justification was simple: to allow pedestrian and automobile traffic to flow freely on downtown streets while also visually exposing the city's architectural jewels for new investors and others to identify and appreciate. But in order to convince street vendors to leave high-rent, investor-friendly areas of the city, the administration would need to hand over control of tens of historic buildings in other less investor-friendly areas of the city to informal vendor organizations as alternative locations for selling, thereby incurring the wrath of INAH.

Specifically, as vendors negotiated with the government for a 'metre per metre' space commitment in return for relocation, they reminded the city's government that they would not abandon downtown streets until they had an equally amenable spot for selling. This in turn set the government on a desperate search to find available properties of a certain size and location, leading to a major review of every free inch of space so as to find new buildings or plazas within the historic centre. Yet many of the available sites held dilapidated buildings and crumbling infrastructures protected by INAH's oversight. Moreover, these buildings and sites needed considerable renovation in order to serve as commercial plazas, a fact which established a very tight deadline by which the city had to deliver on the promise of both street vendor clearance and relocation (Figure 4.7).

In trying to make good on these promises, Ebrard felt forced to choose between undertaking blunt actions that violated INAH guidelines—that is, the movement and relocation of vendors without INAH permission— or enduring months of inflexible legally sanctioned regulations limiting the right to occupy and/or renovate these historic properties, while posting appeals from within the formal bureaucratic channels governed by INAH. Initially, Ebrard took the route of seeking formal permission. But when

Figure 4.7 Renovation of historic commercial street, downtown Mexico City, January 2008. Photograph by Onesimo Flores Dewey.

INAH started dragging its heels by routinely denying permits or holding them for months, Ebrard's patience wore thin. With the acceptance rate of permits plummeting from 100 per cent in 2000 to 67 per cent in 2007, Ebard began to fight back, leading to more open conflict in weekly meetings between the Autoridad and INAH. These tensions ultimately burst into the public eye in the form of the controversy over the Torre. With the October 2007 deadline for removing street vendors nearing as INAH continued to drag its feet in the months immediately following the Torre conflict, the Ebrard team took the controversial step of directly expropriating lots and renovating or rebuilding them for street vendor relocation without INAH permission.

Because some of these buildings were badly maintained, having been abandoned for decades and not designed for commerce, the city also took the unusual step of demolishing them and constructing entirely new spaces as vendor 'plazas'. Although small in number, these acts generated public condemnation from INAH, which in turn inspired Ebrard's opponents in the Asamblea Legislativa and in the well-established historical and preservationist communities to jump on the bandwagon. In January 2008, after a heated public debate and Ebrard's wilful destruction of a key historic convent whose historical patrimony was not under dispute, INAH filed suit against the city. As of the writing of this chapter, the outcome of the trial is still pending.

Conclusions

With a legal verdict still unclear, it is too early to know whether Ebrard's current efforts to balance history and progress in the urban transformation of Mexico City will succeed, or whether he will be defeated. One thing is sure. His plans to help advance the city's economic future while also protecting physical and living elements of its history and culture, both buildings and people, have met with clear institutional and political obstacles. INAH is a major player in this battle. But its wrath has catalyzed wider opposition that does not bode well for Ebard's administration or its plans for the city. As Ebrard is accused of violating the law and destroying national patrimony by removing or refurbishing old sites for street vendor occupancy, political opponents in the PAN and other parties raise questions about the legitimacy of his tenure, despite his gains in clearing the streets of downtown Mexico City.

Complicating matters, Ebrard faces slippage in political support from those who initially stood behind his urban development plans. In 2006 and 2007 his most critical political allies included private sector investors who sought to invest in the cleared areas downtown and street vendors who were promised new locations for their activities. But as of 2008 word was surfacing that the relocated vendors were not making their usual level of profits. This produced grumblings of discontent among street vendor organizations and accusations of selling out to Slim and his property interests, with some sellers using this as justification for venturing back on to central city streets. Some street vendor organizations also started to challenge the vertical organizational control by the political leaders with whom Ebrard negotiated the relocation packages. All these factors have forced Ebrard to proceed much more slowly, with both street clearing and the upscale development end of his plans, something that in turn makes investors nervous and limits the financial support for redevelopment. In short, facing obstacles on a variety of fronts, Ebrard's plans for the city may be as likely to be sunk by a betrayal of loyalties among street vendors and private investors, even before INAH and the courts have their say.

If the future of the city's urban redevelopment remains unknown, how Mexico City got to this point is not. The city and its political leaders have struggled for decades with finding the most politically appropriate mix of history and progress, with any particular balance struck at one moment laying the foundations for subsequent challenge or reversal. Yet despite the shifting political alliances and variable urban outcomes they have produced, several things have remained constant. First, for the past half century the main focus of contention between the forces of history and progress has played itself out over buildings, cultures, monuments and activities nestled downtown in the historic centre. This was so not just because these spaces host a significant concentration of historic patrimony, but also because this area was and remains central to property speculation and development, two aims that increased in importance as the city modernized economically.

Second, each period of conflict gave birth to new institutions to plan or manage downtown development, starting with the Planning Commission in the 1940s and ending with the Autoridad in 2006, with multiple reformulations in between. As new institutions emerged they either replaced or overlapped with old ones, frequently drawing on the same sets of actors (INAH, elected or appointed DF officials, private sector investors) but grouped in different ways with varying degrees of bureaucratic (or private sector) power or influence. Over time, the routine proliferation of new institutions led to fragmentation as well as growing competition and infighting within and between public and private sector forces over control of the agencies charged with making urban policy decisions about the historic centre. This constantly shifting institutional terrain also invited partisan involvement and the super-politicization of urban planning initiatives for the city, a trend that seems to have worsened over time.

Despite the historical continuities, there also have been changes. For one, the policy dilemmas that fuel the tensions between the forces of history and progress have shifted. Transport efficiency, popular housing and a valuation of traditional downtown culture as topics of concern were key in early stages, gradually reducing in importance, and almost dropping off the agenda as decision-making power became ever more focused on high-end property development. Some of this was due to the fact that current INAH regulations ensure that the costs of transforming old buildings into habitable residences remains a financially exorbitant challenge, meaning any renovation in an epoch of rising property values must, almost by definition, be focused on high-rent products. These same constraints have also made it harder for recent administrations, such as Ebrard's, to place topics like popular housing and everyday culture on the downtown planning agenda.

For another, the political and institutional relationship between INAH (and INBA) and Mexico City authorities has shifted over time, moving from a position of insignificance to alliance or mediation to one of antagonism. Before 1972 INAH and INBA had little say in institutions charged with planning downtown areas, and when it was involved, it served as a swing vote in balancing the concerns of cultural preservation and economic progress. In the early 1980s and throughout the 1990s, INAH started to become a more vocal advocate of preservation, dropping the role of mediator or government ally and taking a quasi-oppositional stance against proponents of economic progress when it affected historical buildings and the historical environment of downtown. Starting in 2000 and continuing through the present, INAH and INBA have lost almost all public pretence of negotiation or mediation, becoming an openly hostile force willing and capable of vetoing urban planning actions that might entail some change in the downtown built environment.

Finally, over time we have seen that the physical focus of conflict within and between historic preservationists and Mexico City authorities is shifting in spatial terms, moving from the centremost areas of Perimetro A to the streets and neighbourhoods in Perimetro B, with the latter now serving as a new battleground between city authorities and historic preservationists. The current preoccupation with a larger swathe of urban space is due not just to the strong-armed actions of Ebrard to relocate street vendors in historic buildings in areas outside the traditional historic centre, but also to the successes in redevelopment already achieved in Perimetro A, because of prior investments and initiatives linked to the downtown rescue plan. As the physical site of institutional conflict shifts outward, city authorities are as likely to be in conflict with INBA as INAH, because of the former's legal responsibility over protecting the twentieth-century patrimony. The upshot is that the city is extending its battleground in such a way that it is forced to engage two separate historic preservation agencies simultaneously. This not only makes the fault lines of conflict between preservationists and city officials more bureaucratically complex and divisive than in previous periods; it also generates relatively open institutional warfare over ever larger swathes of the urban built environment.

Ultimately, this is an untenable situation both politically and in terms of urban planning. Any administration seeking to plan for a modernizing metropolis the size and character of Mexico City must be able to offer a comprehensive formulation of urban land use and economic development policies for the city in its entirety. To be successful, any such plan must take into account how changes in certain circumscribed spaces affect other areas, or how support for one set of economic activities affects others, even as it must be able to assess gains and losses both for certain spaces and sectors as well as for the city as a whole. To be constrained by battles over individual buildings and properties is counter-productive, even when the aim is to improve living conditions and standards in the areas surrounding those buildings and properties. Yet if the goal is more ambitious—that is, is to plan for the city as a whole, and to manage the balance of history and progress as Mexico City continues its path to a modern future—then the bureaucratic battles that threaten to bring the current mayor to his knees will be fatal. The forces of preservation will have won. But at what cost?

The main loser in any such scenario will be the city and its people, who are held hostage to a bureaucratic quagmire that will advance neither the aims of historic preservation nor the course of economic progress. Glorious Mexico City, once known as the city of palaces, would then be facing the same stalemated situation it confronted more than two decades ago, when I first started studying the politics of urban development three decades ago. How sad to consider that a city I once characterized as 'worse than a planner's nightmare . . .[and] a depressing testament to administrative chaos' might not have moved much beyond this longstanding state of affairs.[3] Despite the obvious political gains produced by democratization and despite the creative investments and new programmes that have produced a partial regeneration of its built environment, Mexico City may still be stuck in time, honouring a glorious past and willing to embrace a promising new future but unable to move forcefully in either direction without imploding into bureaucratic or political conflict.

Note. Thanks to Onesimo Flores Dewey, doctoral candidate at MIT and a principal assistant on this project, for archival work and participating in interviews

[3] Diane E. Davis, *Urban Leviathan: Mexico City in the Twentieth Century* (Philadelphia, Temple University Press, 1994), p. 2.

for this study. I also thank Dr Margarita González Gamio and Dr Alejandra Moreno Toscano for alerting me to the complexity of this issue and for their willingness to share their views. Additional thanks go to the following persons, who shared information about historic preservation in Mexico City: Alfonso de María and Saul Alcántara from the INAH, Ramón Vargas and Dolores Martínez from the INBA, Leticia Bonifaz from the office of the Mayor, Enrique Díaz Cuervo from the Asamblea Legislativa, as well as Rene Coulomb, Cecilia Barraza and José Castillo. All the analysis and interpretation are the sole responsibility of the author, and do not reflect the official (or unofficial) views of any of the informants.

Further reading

Cory, Steve and Ray Webb, *Daily Life in Aztec and Modern Mexico City* (Minneapolis, MN: Lerner Publishing Group, 1999).

Cross, John C., *Informal Politics: Street Vendors and the State in Mexico City* (Palo Alto: Stanford University Press, 1998).

Davis, Diane E., *Urban Leviathan: Mexico City in the Twentieth Century* (Philadelphia: Temple University Press, 1994).

————, 'Reverberations: Mexico City's 1985 Earthquake and the Transformation of the Capital', in *The Resilient City*, ed. Lawrence Vale and Tom Campanella (Oxford: Oxford University Press, 2004), pp. 255–80.

————, 'Conflict, Cooperation, and Convergence: Globalization and the Politics of Downtown Development in Mexico City', *Research in Political Sociology* 15 (2006): 143–78.

García Cortés, Adrián, *La reforma urbana de México: crónica de la Comisión de Planificación del Distrito Federal* (Mexico: Bay Gráfica y Ediciones, 1972).

Herzog, Lawrence A., *Return to the Center: Culture, Public Space, and City Building in a Global Era* (Austin: University of Texas Press, 2006).

Ward, Peter, *Mexico City.* 2nd edn (New York: John Wiley and Sons, 1998).

III
CULTURE

5. THE POETIC CITY
From the Consecration to the Degradation of Spring: the Poet in the Street
VICENTE QUIRARTE

> Every action has a meaning. For an artist and for God, everyday familiar reality is an allegorical poem. Every man lives, day by day, an Odyssey, on his way to the office or the bar. Life is not what it seems to be. It is not the daily mediocrity of an insignificant being, for in those mediocrities, art may find the invisible map of an epic poem.
>
> René Albérès

> Nic cuicailacatzoa cohuayotli.
> In tecpan nicquixtiz,
> an ya tonmochin,
> quin icuac tonmochin in otiyaque ye Mictlan.
> In yuh ca zan tictlanehuico.

> [With songs I encircle the community
> Which I will bring into the palace,
> There we will all be,
> Until we have gone to the region of the dead.
> Thus we have been loaned to one other.][1]

These are words that were lived and written by Temilotzin of Tlaltelolco, poet and warrior, friend of Cuauhtémoc, the last Aztec Emperor, who chose to die on his own, after being defeated, before being dominated and humiliated by the conquerors. This poem synthesizes the principal values of the city of Tenochtitlan, the capital of the Aztec Empire, which based its spiritual greatness upon flowers and song.

According to ancient native traditions, a city could not be considered to be completely founded before a song house had been built, and our poet underlines the function of the shared word: fraternity, a preoccupation with the passing of time, the certainty that the transcendent meaning of our

---

[1] Miguel León Portilla, *Fifteen Poets of the Aztec World* (Norman: University of Oklahoma Press, 1992), pp. 194–5.

presence on earth is to give ourselves to each other. This was one of the main points that were taught to the young priests at the *calmecac*: 'They carefully learnt the songs known as the god's songs, written in books. And they carefully learned the counting of days, the book of dreams and the book of years.'[2] Temilotzin's testimony is doubly dramatic. He came from a warrior-priest society that dominated all the neighbouring towns, the very mention of which was enough to terrify their enemies. But the song of the poet also belonged to a time when there was a harmonious alliance between poetry and the city. The urban landscape and nature was a perpetual coronation of spring, its equilibrium never altered. Established in a place that would not seem to be the best location to found a city, the choice was the result of prophecy and faith in destiny. The latter was so great and intense that in very few years the original primitive village became the splendid, admired and feared city of Tenochtitlan. In 1469, a few years before the fall of the city into the hands of the Spanish conquerors, King Nezahualcóyotl celebrated the region's transparency of air, which would acquire the status of legend with the passage of time.

'La ciudad sobre el lago'

La niebla se tiende sobre nosotros:
Que broten nuevas flores bellas
y estén en vuestras manos entretejidas
¡será vuestro canto y vuestra palabra!

Flores de luz erguidas abren sus corolas
donde se tiende el musgo acuático, aquí en México,
plácidamente están ensanchándose,
y en medio del musgo y de los matices
está tendida la ciudad de Tenochtitlan:
La extiende y la hace florecer el dios:
Tiene sus ojos fijos en sitios como éste,
los tiene fijos en medio del lago.

Columnas de turquesa se hicieron aquí,
en el inmenso lago se hicieron columnas.
Es el dios que sustenta la ciudad,
y lleva en sus brazos a Anáhuac en la inmensa laguna.

['The City on the Lake'

Mist unfolds over us:
Let beautiful new flowers bloom
And lay within thy entwined hands
It shall be thy song and thy word!

[2] Jacques Soustelle, *La vida cotidiana de los aztecas en vísperas de la conquista*, 10th edn (México City: Fondo de Cultura Económica, 1983), p. 233.

Flowers of light open their corollas
Where the watery moss lies, here in México,
They spread out placidly,
And amidst the moss and the hues
The city of Tenochtitlan lies:
The god extends it and makes it bloom:
His eyes are fixed on places like this,
They are fixed on the middle of the lake.

Turquoise columns were made here,
Columns were made in the immense lake.
It is the god who sustains the city,
And carries Anáhuac in his arms, in the immense lagoon.][3]

And in 1982, in his poem 'Third Tenochtitlan', Eduardo Lizalde traces out a map, seen from above, of the new monster engendered by modernity.

'Tercera Tenochtitlan' (Fragmento)
Sobre el valle que aúlla
Fauces de un dios alza el aire sus torres
De Alturas pasajeras e invisibles
Su contrafuerte frágil de briznas microscópicas
Su nebulosa de insectos

Al centro la gran mancha de petróleo o tinta
Un Rorchsach la falena nictálope
De la ciudad velada por su niebla letal
Un continente de aeronauta pelusa
Un grajo inmenso que se petrifica a la mitad del vuelo

[Over the howling valley
A god's jaws lift in the air its towers
Of invisible and transient heights
Its fragile buttress of microscopic blade remnants
Its insect nebulae

A great stain of oil or ink at the centre
A Rorschach nyctalope moth
Of the city guarded by its lethal fog
An aeronautic continent of down
An immense rook petrified in mid-flight.][4]

Five centuries separate these poets. Five centuries in which the harmony between man and his environment has deteriorated. The words of

---

[3] Nezahualcóyotl, ''La ciudad sobre el lago', in Emmanuel Carballo and José Luis Martínez (eds), *Páginas sobre la Ciudad de México (1469–1987)* (Mexico City: Consejo de la Crónica de la Ciudad de México, 1988), p.31.

[4] Eduardo Lizalde, 'Tercera Tenochtitlan', in *Memoria del tigre* (Mexico City: Fondo de Cultura Económica, 1995), p. 317.

Netzalhualcóyotl are diaphanous, colourful and in communion with the Giver of Life. Lizalde's words are hostile, chaotic and 'the Devil's script'. 'Todo tiempo pasado fue mejor ' ('All past time was better') the founders of Mexico once declared when witnessing the first transformations of their proud space. On seeing community wisdom transformed into tyranny, democracy into authoritarian monarchy, they must have yearned for their paradisiacal existence, where the bounty of the Valley of Mexico was once lavished upon the city.

Writing reveals both enlightenment and disaster. In the midst of both extremes, the poet embarks upon the search for permanence and survival in the city. T. S. Eliot talks about an 'Unreal City', mentioning a ghostly London, sunk in fog. At the same time, and at the other side of the ocean, the Mexican poet José Gorostiza points out the factors that seemingly divorce the individual from the city: 'Man does not live, as he once did, in empathy with nature. The sky no longer enters the city's composition in big blue chunks. Prisoner of a room, gorged in silence and hungry for communication, he has become—island man—a solitude surrounded by people. His garden is in the rug's discoloured flowers, his birds the radio receiver, his spring in the fan's vanes, his love in the tears of the woman mending clothes in a corner.'[5]

The city is a text, and we all contribute to its writing. The brief odyssey of crossing it daily is as important as the heroic epiphanies that crown our adventure. The poet, like an urban planner, is a professional reader of his or her environment, an initiate capable of translating its changes and emotions. The poet is the emotional biographer of the city, as exemplified by Octavio Paz throughout the various stages of his writing: in his youth, he used the classical form of the sonnet for the poem entitled 'City Twilights'; in his maturity, he relied on free verse and chaotic enumeration, verbal forms that chimed with the chaotic city of the end of the century. In the following pages, I shall attempt to share with you the ways in which the poet and poetry have traced the invisible map of Mexico City, and how this initiate's language protects and strengthens memories while also helping us to live through each day with increased dignity.

Through three centuries of colonial rule, proud Tenochtitlan lost its name and had imposed on it that of New Spain. During those years vari-ous alliances between poetry and the city were made, where the former was part of the spectacle and the poet took on the dishonourable role of jester.

---

[5] José Gorostiza, 'Notas sobre poesía', in *Poesía* (Mexico City: Fondo de Cultura Económica, 1964), pp. 22–3.

Authors would write poems inscribed on triumphal arches built when a new viceroy first entered the city. Most of these have been forgotten, but not those of Sor Juana Inés de la Cruz, whose poetry was the most important of her time, and which, centuries after they were written, we still find illuminating. Sor Juana never wrote a poem in which Mexico City was a protagonist, but her biography is the best example of a writer who faces all obstacles in order to become an active member of the *polis*. The difficulty she encountered, as a woman who wished to think, study and write, led her to the convent. From it, and notwithstanding it, she waged her exemplary battle. At the centre of the ancient city, the walls of the Hieronymus Order's convent still stand, where—in the words of the poet Francisco de Quevedo—the nun's 'enamoured dust' lies. The lessons she taught us were many, and one can be highlighted in this exploration of the poet and the city: her opposition to all the canons imposed by a rigid and authoritarian society, a disobedience that took her to the heart of the enlightened city. In her cell room she collected one of the most important personal libraries of her time and in it the most brilliant and polemical words of the Golden Age were written.

The greatest poetic description of the baroque city can be found in *Grandeza mexicana* (*Mexican Greatness*), an extensive poem by Bernardo de Balbuena. Though he was born in Spain, it was in Mexico that he developed as a writer and wrote the majority of his work. The poem appeared in 1604, when Miguel de Cervantes was about to deliver *Don Quixote* to the printers and when William Shakespeare wrote *Troilus and Cressida*, one of his most obscure and intense plays. The Mexican poet aimed to describe the beauties of the capital at the height of its splendour, when its buildings and organization were admired by locals and outsiders alike. The argument of the poem can be found in the first stanza:

> De la famosa México el asiento,
> origen y grandeza de edificios,
> caballos, calles, trato, cumplimiento,
> letras, virtudes, variedad de oficios,
> regalos, ocasiones de contento,
> primavera inmortal y sus indicios,
> gobierno ilustre, religión, estado,
> todo en este discurso está cifrado.

> [Of famed Mexico the seat,
> origin and greatness of buildings
> horses, streets, manners, fulfilment
> words, virtues, variety of trades,
> gifts, happy occasions,

immortal spring and its signs,
illustrious government, religion, state,
all is numbered in this discourse.][6]

The poem leaves no doubt as to the greatness of the city, which the British traveller Thomas Gage once described as 'one of the largest of the World considering the extension of the houses of Spaniards and Indians'.[7] Balbuena evokes a highly concentrated empire, this jewel beyond the ocean, and he exclusively praises its splendour. However, there are no human contrasts or common passions in the poem. Blood, sweat and tears are lacking. The monumentality of the city's buildings, the temperate climate and the harmony of the city seem to exist independent of its inhabitants. But there was another story, both marginal and secret. While the opulence of the capital's privileged classes was very visible, the city also gave birth to an extensive 'court of miracles': the Indian neighbourhoods that had been banished from the original plan. Dorantes de Carranza includes in his *Sumaria relación* a piece by an anonymous poet, also written in 1604, which offers a contrast to Balbuena's poem, painting another portrait of New Spain through its colourful inhabitants:

Minas sin plata, sin verdad mineros,
mercaderes por ellas codiciosos,
caballeros de serlo deseosos,
con mucha presunción bodegoneros.
Mujeres que se venden por dineros,
dejando a los mejores muy quejosos;
calles, casas, caballos muy hermosos;
muchos amigos, pocos verdaderos.
Negros que no obedecen a sus señores;
señores que no mandan en su casa;
jugando sus mujeres noche y día;
colgados del virrey mil pretensores;
tïanguis, almoneda, behetría. . .
Aquesto, en suma, en esta ciudad pasa.

[Mines without silver, truthless miners,
merchants greedy for them,
gentlemen desiring to be so,
upstart mongers.
Women selling themselves for money,

---

[6] Bernardo de Balbuena, *Grandeza mexicana*, ed. Luis Adolfo Domínguez (Mexico City: Editorial Porrúa, 1971), p. 59.

[7] Serge Gruzinski, 'La ciudad de México en 1600: una capital americana en los albores de globalización', in *La ciudad de México en los fines de siglo (XV-XX)*, ed. Manuel Ramos Medina (Mexico City: Centro de Estudios de Historia Condumex, Grupo Carso, 2001), p. 60.

leaving the best protesting;
streets, homes, beautiful horses;
many friends, few true.
Blacks who do not obey their masters,
masters with no authority in their house;
their women out playing night and day;
a thousand pretenders hanging on to the viceroy;
marketplace, auction house, disorder. . .
This is, in sum, what passes in this city.][8]

As described in one of the previous verses, New Spain's capital was teeming with 'pretenders' who would hang around the viceroy in the hope of obtaining a high post, their claims not based on their own merits or culture but rather on being the descendents of the first conquistadors. The city then, a place of both order and festivity, pleasure and aloofness, bears many similarities with the city today. As Serge Gruzinski has noted in his splendid biography of Mexico City, the nascent seventeenth century witnessed a first great surge of globalization.

The eighteenth century was a century of prose, and Mexico City was no exception. Numerous texts analysed, scientifically and statistically, the situation of the empire's capital. The independence of American nations is pure and active romanticism, and with it comes the supremacy of imagination and the first person, as well as the discovery of popular culture and citizens' action. The poet becomes a solitary explorer of the street, a *flâneur*, a wanderer, whose main occupation is to find the meaning of each one of his steps. One day in 1836, a young twenty-two-year-old named Guillermo Prieto walks out onto the street. He has not yet read William Hazlitt, yet his finely tuned instinct tells him that walking the city is the most complete way of reading it, possessing it, and sharing it. He walks, and as he translates each step he takes, he writes his first urban chronicle, a delightful sensuous journey through the city, from the first bells ringing from the churches to the last shouts of the night vendors hawking their wares in an intense and discordant symphony. The poet will, as Edgar Allan Poe discovered in 'The Man of the Crowd', be part of a new order that is born out of industrial society, a society that, overnight, had modified the concepts of time and space. We can see these changes reflected in the work of Mexican authors, but they echo in other languages and other parts of the world: Charles Baudelaire, whose *petits poèmes en prose* prove that a city changes faster than a heartbeat; Charles Dickens and his orphans give new meaning to London's streets; Victor Hugo's young rebels raising the barricades; Nathaniel Hawthorne's 'Wakefield', shipwrecked on the great city's hostile

---

[8] Emmanuel Carballo y José Luis Martínez, *Páginas sobre la Ciudad de México*, p. 85.

ocean. It is a universal phenomenon and it is astonishing to see the parallels between authors who, without knowing or having read each other, share the same love–hate relationship with the modern city.

This is Mexico's nineteenth century. A time of heroes and scoundrels, muses and poets, of heightened virtues and hyperbolic flaws. A time for insurrections and revolutions, civil wars and foreign invasions (Figure 5.1). A time for yellow-gloved corsairs, with redemptive projects and remedies as radical as they were fallible, as impossible as they were miraculous. A time for the military to change, from one day to the next, the map of the city, while they parade their medals alongside the *soutaines* and cassocks that defend their privileges; a time of civilians led by an Indian named Benito Juárez, whose frockcoat became a symbol of authority; a time of civilians that endow the fledgling nation with institutions, individual guarantees and with tools for progress. This is the nineteenth century. It finds expression in the street vendors' cries, Indians offering their wares from the village of Tacuba; in the same noxious and corrupt air where a Frenchman called Meroliock spoke in empty and entangled baroque prose: his name would later be given to verbose street vendors: *merolicos*. It is heralded by citizens that leap, overnight, from anonymity onto the stage of History. Men who are synonymous with the city, who take to the streets and recover their place in the world. A time in which individuals participate directly, actively, in decision-making and formulate political myths and social metaphors that define us to this day. Mexico's nineteenth century put up for sale by scoundrels. Offered to the highest bidder without scruple. Saved from ruin by its miracles and secular martyrs, by its thinkers and by those executed by firing squads.

At a time when the concept of nationalism was at its inception, the poet becomes an educator, an authority figure. The street is the stage where this slow process of formation takes place. In an illiterate society, political speech becomes a great mural of words that offers a panoramic view of history from the distant past to this very moment. Guillermo Prieto, Ignacio Ramírez, Francisco Zarco, Ignacio Manuel Altamirano, all men of letters, become the men of action who create the new city, in accordance with liberal ideals, from the public square, the theatre, or from parliament. The other great urban genre of the nineteenth century, apart from oratory, would be the chronicle, the description of customs that privileged speech, customs and everyday behaviour, the vices and virtues of its inhabitants. And even though both genres, the chronicle and oratory, are written in prose, they would not communicate with us so strongly if their authors had not been, above all else, poets, if they did not have total mastery over the weight and nuance of every word and every symbol. Among all these names, Guillermo Prieto was the great heroic bard, but also the historian

Figure 5.1 Carl Nebel, *American Troops in Mexico City*, 13 September 1847.

of those without history. His most significant book, *La musa callejera* (*Muse of the Street,* 1883), reveals even in its title this interest in the intense and rowdy life of the city where he was born, and which he untiringly explored throughout the almost eighty years of his life.

This nineteenth century of urban exploration in Mexico City ends symbolically with the young woman in Manuel Gutiérrez Najera's 'La duquesa de Job' ('The Duchess of Job'), who, alone and on foot, crosses the boulevards of Mexico City armed only with her beauty and the terrible efficiency of her high heels. The slow conquest of the city by women is speeded up by the Mexican Revolution that ushered in the twentieth century. The city that emerges from the Revolution witnesses a radical change in the use of the urban space. At a time when the armed phase of the movement is nearly over, women want something more than to be good *soldaderas*—fellow soldiers and helpmates—to their men. They press for rights denied to them by a virile, authoritarian and paternalistic homeland, often becoming the subjects of courageous works of art. The female body wages its own war for autonomy at a time when the Revolution, resolutely machista, persecuted its manly homosexuals and expected unconditional acquiescence from its women. With the Revolution, women express their desire to become active in the construction of Mexico, and also in the construction of a room of their own.

In 1921, Ramón López Velarde wrote the poem 'La suave patria ('Gentle Homeland'): in it, he embraces the nation and declares his love passionately and irreverently, in terms so fresh and new that we can still quote it unashamedly. Before this, Saturnino Herrán painted his series of exuberant *criolla* women, in which he offers the visual equivalent of a healthy feminine country, a joyous and splendid looking female in the sunlight. López Velarde's poetry and Herrán's paintings fill the stage and are defining moments of a period—like the morning in which Tina Modotti lies down naked on a rooftop in the Condesa neighbourhood to be lovingly, obsessively, photographed by Edward Weston; like the moment in which Carmen Mondragón turns into Nahui Olín to her lover's terror and ecstasy; like the day when the actress Clementina Otero receives a letter from her poet admirer declaring 'I am dying from being without you'; like the moment when an adolescent girl named Frida Kahlo courageously approached the enormous figure of Diego Rivera, who was giving pictorial life to the walls of the city, in an art crusade that was another Renaissance.

The Revolution opens up new streets, broad and spacious, that imitate those seen by the Sonora politicians in the United States. Salvador Novo mirrors the optimistic spirit of the post-revolutionary city in his book *Nueva grandeza mexicana* (1946) (*New Mexican Greatness*). The future official chronicler of the city where he was born, Novo takes us, his readers, along with him and shows us the different phases of the city's development, the places to live, find pleasure, love and death. Nevertheless, parallel to this powerful and progressive city, which was still little more than a big town, there was another Mexico City, intimate and secret, fashioned by Novo and his fellow writers, the generation known as *Los Contemporáneos*: the city below the surface, the city of latent desire. One of the clearest examples is that of Xavier Villaurrutia, in the poems found in his book *Nostalgia de la muerte* (*Nostalgia for Death*, 1938). The night he sings of is the night of the romantics but also the secret night of post-revolutionary Mexico, closer and even more tangible, the space inhabited by hunters and insomniacs, adulterers and the suicidal. If Villaurrutia's night is a tense space in which man discovers he is bereft because he is alone with himself, there is an immediate correspondence with surrealism, not as a technique but as a way of life. The key can be found in the word *desire*; the night is the place where a demi-monde of initiates can pursue their activities. The night offers freedom. But the night also ensnares and grips in its jaws even the wisest and strongest men and women. One very fertile area of study is the relationship of between our poets and popular songs, especially the *bolero*, an urban genre par excellence. We can glimpse this influence in these lines written by Villaurrutia:

> 'Amor condusse noi ad una morte'
>
> Amar es una angustia, una pregunta,
> una suspensa y luminosa duda;
> es una querer saber todo lo tuyo
> y a la vez un temor de al fin saberlo.
>
> To love is an anguish, a question,
> A suspended and luminous doubt;
> It is wanting to know all of you
> And the fear of, in the end, knowing it all.[9]

A contemporary of the aforementioned poets, Manuel Maples Arce was the founder of the vanguard movement known as Estridentismo. His poem *Metropolis*, translated by John Dos Passos, is a historical milestone since it was the first book by a Mexican poet to be published in another language. It appeared in New York in 1929, published by T. S. Books Company.

> Here is my poem
> Gruff
> Multiple
> Of the new city.
> O city all tense
> with cables and strains
> all humming with motors and wings.
> simultaneous explosion
> of new theories
> a little beyond
> in the diagram of space
> Whitman and Turner
> a little this side
> of Maples Arce.[10]

As Dickens taught us in the title of one of his most beloved novels, what we say or write about of a city is always *A Tale of Two Cities*. The twentieth century was no exception. One is shaped by the discourse of empire, the discourse of Big Brother, a new conquest that in the name of progress builds cardboard houses with satellite dishes and uproots the former inhabitants, building walls that segregate city life. The other is the poet's discourse, subversive and at times painful, but necessary for us to become

---

[9] Xavier Villaurrutia, 'Amor condusse noi ad una morte', in *Obras,* ed. Alí Chamucero (Mexico City: Fondo de Cultura Económica, 1966), p.76.
[10] Manuel Maples Arce, *Metropolis*, trans. John Dos Passos (New York, T.S. Books Company, 1929), p.9.

aware of the daily chaos we live in. Let me quote a poem written at the end of the twentieth century by Francisco Hernández, the title of which I have included in my own chapter title: 'The Degradation of Spring'. The traditional image of the romantic poet as a new God, observing from his solitary look-out post a rough sea of clouds, is here replaced by the poet as city dweller observing the dawning of a new day from one of the many jerry-built buildings that have replaced historical architecture:

'La degradación de la primavera'

I

La he mirado con lástima en los últimos meses.
Estoy en un décimo piso y hasta acá llegan los bramidos
de las perforadoras, el rumor de los automóviles y
gemidos de perros negándose a morir.

La observo fijamente, trato de ver el sol entre sus brumas. A tan temprana hora, la ciudad es un paquidermo que bosteza.

II

Huele mal la ciudad. Con la llegada de la primavera
han florecido las alcantarillas. En medio del polvo y el ozono
brotan vislumbres de jacarandas, alfanjes de colorines y un olor
penetrante a naranjas podridas.

III

Abajo hay policías, boleros, enfermeras, enanos, asaltantes. Llamas de incendios salen por las ventanas y el ulular de las sirenas anuncia el señorío de la violencia.

Aquí en el décimo piso, los muertos caminamos con recelo, angustiados, alertas, no sea que nos vayan a matar de nuevo.

IV

Las azoteas son patios elevados, nidos de gatas, el último rincón de las macetas.
En jaulas se destiñen sábanas, manteles y camisas de fuerza. No sopla el viento y un anuncio de cerveza se desploma. Una viejita lucha con avispas imaginarias. Un ciclista recuerda las mañanas en que se veían los volcanes, se distrae y una combi le parte las costillas.

V

Hay más antenas parabólicas que árboles. Zopilotes pequeños, muy parecidos a palomas, sobrevuelan las calles en busca de migajas o excremento.
Los cilindros de gas empollan su potencia. Los tinacos tienen la boca seca y esperan, temblorosos, la temporada de la lluvia ácida.

VI

No dejan de sonar los teléfonos. Otros muertos nos llaman desde lejanos cementerios verticales.

Afuera, el color dominante es el gris. Aquí en el décimo piso, nada tiene color, salvo los labios de las muertas.

Me asomo nuevamente para admirar la primavera.

Rodeados de basura se besan los amantes y se aparean las ratas.

[The Degradation of Spring

I

I have seen her with pity these last few months.
I am on a tenth floor and even here I can listen to the bellows
of drills, the sound of automobiles and
the groans of dogs that refuse to die.

I look at her carefully, I try to see the sun amidst her haze. At such an early hour, the city
Is a yawning pachyderm.

II

The city smells bad. With the arrival of spring
The sewers have bloomed. Amidst the dust and ozone
Glimpses of jacarandas, coloured scimitars and a pervasive odour of rotten oranges.

III

Down there, police officers, bootblacks, nurses, midgets, muggers. Flames lick out of windows and the sirens' ululating call announce the domain of violence.

Here on the tenth floor, the dead walk cautiously, in anguish, ever alert, it could well be we shall all be killed again.

IV

The rooftops are raised patios, cat nests, the pots' last available corner. Inside the cages, sheets, tablecloths and straitjackets are discoloured. There is no wind and a beer billboard plummets. An old lady fights off imaginary wasps. A cyclist remembers the mornings when the volcanoes could be seen and, distracted, is hit by a combi passenger bus that breaks his ribs.

V

There are far more satellite dishes than trees. Small vultures, very similar to doves, fly over the streets searching for crumbs or excrement. The gas tanks nurse their power. The cisterns are dry mouthed and await, trembling, the acid rain season.

VI

The telephones don't stop ringing. Other dead people call us from far-off vertical cemeteries.
Outside, the predominant colour is grey. Here, on the tenth floor, All is colourless except for the lips of the dead women.

I look out again to admire the spring.

Surrounded by rubbish, the lovers kiss and the rats mate.][11]

Francisco Hernández' poem seems to condemn us, inevitably, to the apocalypse. However, in each of his implacable and surprising metaphors, there is a place for dark humour, a very Mexican humour which is one of the weapons that have helped us survive. *The Vision of the Vanquished* is the title of a book in which Miguel León-Portilla gathers testimonies of the fall of this ancient city. In the burgeoning twenty-first century, the inhabitants of one the most populated cities on the planet seem to share a similar vision. To foreign eyes, and to our own, we seem to be losing the battle against a new conqueror: the empire of manipulated information, consumerism, domestic violence, the nine-millimetre gun that has become in part of our city's daily information. Efraín Huerta, the city's great poet, wrote: 'We walk, as if under cypress trees, under the long shadow of fear . . .There is no respect for even the air we breathe.'[12] His words were written in 1956 when the term 'ecology' had yet to become part of our daily life, and when walking the streets was doubly heroic in the face of government forces repressing political militancy. Today, the shadow is even more threatening. We are no longer waiting for the barbarians. When we look at ourselves in the mirror we see the weapons and the armour of the warrior we have become, facing the challenges of each new day.

The city was formed to replace nomadic existence and to concentrate the power and the progress of civilization. More particularly, in Lewis Mumford's words: 'Historically the city begins in the village—a group of households attached to the soil. Here nurture and neighbourly cooperation are the two basic elements; the limited horizon and a repetitive routine give to the growing child security and to the adult the basis of social solidarity, like mindedness.'[13] From this point of view, ours has ceased to be the *City without Walls* that the poet W. H. Auden yearned for as utopia. Mexico City has not only increased the number and reach of its walls, but also gates have

---

[11] Francisco Hernández, 'La degradación de la primavera', in *Poesía reunida (1974–1994)* (Mexico City: Universidad Nacional Autónoma de México, 1996), pp. 558–9.
[12] Efraín Huerta, 'Avenida Juárez', in *Poesía , 1935–1968* (Mexico City: Joaquín Mortiz, 1968), pp. 178–9, 181.
[13] Lewis Mumford, 'What is a City?', in *The Lewis Mumford Reader,* ed. Donald L. Miller (New York: Pantheon Books, 1986), p.105

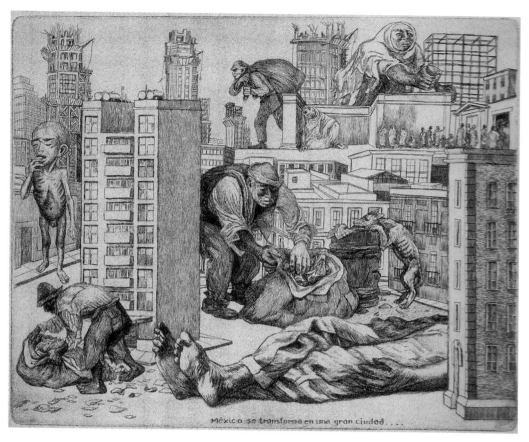

Figure 5.2 Alfredo Zalce. *Mexico Becomes a Great City* (1947). From *Pasado y presente del Centro Histórico*. México City: Fomento Cultural Banamex, 1993, p. 96.

become a prominent feature. Initially there for protection, they have become, imperceptibly, cages that increasingly isolate us from beautiful mornings, the patrimonial sun, the democracy of poisoned air.

We are paying the price of having given birth to a Megalopolis (Figure 5.2): the monster rebels, sooner or later, against its creator, and we must slowly win back the initial harmony. Devouring she-wolf, nurturing mother, in her womb there is still a place for miracles or catastrophe, for actions or dreams. I shall end with one of the many examples that contemporary Mexico City offers of people not feeling defeated by the city and still less falling prey to a sense of hatred that the majority of its inhabitants seem to hold for it. This is an interdisciplinary work by Ana Álvarez, Valentina Rojas Loa and Christian von Wissel, who in 2006 produced a book of words and images entitled *Citámbulos: Guía de asombros de la Ciudad de México*. (*Citywalkers: A Guide to the Wonderment of Mexico City*). All cities have their implicit mysteries, that are shared to some extent, their domestic rituals, but also their curtains, their doors, their glass walls that must deciphered by all those who live the city in another way, deciphered by the *citámbulo,* city-walker.

Mexico City is not one but several cities. Because of its social and economic diversity, there are areas that will never become shared spaces. The city-walker is the avowed enemy of the tourist. Even from its root, *tour,* the word tourist implies a form of domestication. If they are both lucky and have perseverance, tourists can change and be adopted by the space they visit, the contradictory impulse of travelling and space notwithstanding. This heterodox guide is faithful to its own principles, one of which is closely akin to the sense of surprise espoused by the surrealists: the chance encounter between an umbrella and a sewing machine on an operating table.

A city-walker is, first and foremost, an explorer. An image hunter. The city-walker declares himself a faithful follower of knights on horseback, but in the manner of the knight from La Mancha, Don Quixote. He must be attuned to seeing castles where others see inns; giants where the non-initiated would simply see windmills. A city-walker enshrines mistrust as one of his most precious talismans. Though he reads and feeds from secondary sources, his text is the territory that he deciphers. Therefore he eschews any chronicle that might be full of clichés or exoticism. The city-walker is a two-legged animal and at times he also walks on all fours: he goes into the depth of the sewers in the dark, scraping his hands and knees. He lives the city through all six senses. The city-walker sees the city as Dr Caligari's new cabinet: none of its walls, beings, objects, events, realities, moments are the same as any other. All share kinship in the fact that they are territories where no one has ever planted their flag before.

Another way to avoid defeat, in our daily urban life, is through the permanence and transformation of the word. In this sense, Rubén Bonifaz Nuño, the greatest of our living poets, insists: 'The poet, as a man, keeps faith with himself basically by being part of the city; a place and source of solidarity, the city is the setting for sensual love and fraternal communication. In order to protect, preserve and improve it, men and women respond with pleasure and pride to its call to arms, and see this as the greatest honour that life can bestow.'[14]

In a city under siege where the attackers give the order that all the inhabitants except one must be killed, the community will chose the poet as the solitary survivor. 'Great power brings with it great responsibility', one

[14] Rubén Bonifaz Nuño, *Antología de la poesía griega* (Mexico City: Universidad Nacional Autónoma de México, 1989), p. 17

of the urban heroes of our times has stated. Since he has the gift of journeying in and out of madness, the poet has the responsibility to tell and sing the stories of others. By naming despair, we transcend it. According to the ancient annals of the foundation of Mexico City it was said that: 'As long as the world exists, the honour and glory of Mexico-Tenochtitlan should never be forgotten.' We bear these words in mind over and over again, when either nature or man has radically altered the urban balance. The student movement of 1968 and the earthquake of 1985 created a before and after. In the first of these great milestones, youthful imagination took over the streets and made them pulse in a different way. It reminded the city that it was alive, that we should be realists and demand the impossible. The earthquake opened a deep wound. In addition to the numerous deaths and material losses, the quake also brought to light the city's worst sins and its best virtues. Better than anyone, José Emilio Pacheco has described these in his elegy, 'Las ruinas de México':

> Para los que ayudaron, gratitud eterna, homenaje.
> Cómo olvidar—joven desconocida, muchacho anónimo,
> anciano jubilado, madre de todos, héroes sin nombre –
> que ustedes fueron desde el primer minuto de espanto
> a detener la muerte con la sangre
> de sus manos y de sus lágrimas;
> con la certeza
> de que el otro soy yo, yo soy el otro,
> y tu dolor, mi prójimo lejano,
> es mi más hondo sufrimiento.
>
> Para todos ustedes acción de gracias perenne.
> Porque si el mundo no se vino abajo
> en su integridad sobre México
> fue porque lo asumieron
> en sus espaldas ustedes,
> héroes plurales, honor del género humano,
> único orgullo de cuanto sigue en pie sólo por ustedes.

['The ruins of Mexico'

For those that helped, eternal gratitude, honour.
How to forget—unknown girl, anonymous boy,
Elderly pensioner, everyone's mother, nameless heroes-
That you were from this frightened moment
Staunching death with the blood
Of your hands and tears;
With the certainty
That the other is myself, that I am the other,
And your pain, my distant self,
Is my deepest suffering.

To all of you eternal thanksgiving.
Because if the world didn't fall to pieces
In all its wholeness over Mexico
It was because you
Took it on your own backs,
Plural heroes, honour of the human race,
Singular pride of all that remains standing only because of you.][15]

To read a city, especially one in which we have been born, is an act of love and understanding. Since the city is a changing creature, both lethal and generous, we are unsure—once we decipher the signs—if our daring will someday allow us to know her, question her, refute her. Or love her against all odds. We read the city as we walk, as we discover her unknown face, when we trace the map of our journey through her, when she allows us to return home and dream of once again taking up the daily struggle: to defend and gain our place in her incessant representation. The city as a great house; the house as a small city, as envisaged by the Renaissance architect.

Living a city is both necessary and inevitable. Even if we hate it, though we can find both similarities and differences in our love and loathing. Efraín Huerta's 'Declaración de odio' ('Declaration of Hate'), is one the most intense love poems to the capital. Living this city seems to be an ever more difficult task. It is easy to fall prey to an immediate negative reaction: looking to find ways to avoid, however fleetingly, the overall sense of impending disaster. However, sooner or later, humiliated and shamed, convinced or still sceptical, for mysterious reasons we return to her, the impossible, unfaithful, insufferable one. The inevitable City of Mexico, noble and loyal, despite us. In its almost 700 years of existence we have, as have the elements, destroyed our city many times. With identical passion and energy we have rebuilt it. We cannot finish her off, which only testifies to her lineage. But it also testifies to her inhabitants' mettle, though we might be the first to deny such a responsibility and privilege. Every moment offers the possibility of an epiphany: the astonishment of a voice in the midst of blindness. Never before as now do we need the anonymous hero whose daily actions consecrate, elevate and dignify the space. For this reason, reading the city is a way of defending it. Holding it aloft every day while living it.

Note.   Translated by Paloma Díaz Abreu.

---

[15] José Emilio Pacheco, 'Las ruinas de México. Elegía del retorno', in *Tarde o temprano. (Poemas 1958–2000)*, 3rd rev. edn (Mexico City: Fondo de Cultura Económica, 2000), p. 315.

Further Reading

Carreto, Héctor, *La región menos transparente. La Ciudad de México en la poesía* (Mexico City: Gobierno de la Ciudad de México-Editorial Colibrí, 2005).

Gruzinski, Serge, *Histoire de Mexico* (Paris: Libraire Arthème Fayard, 1996).

Iturriaga de la Fuente, José, *Anecdotario de viajeros extranjeros en México. Siglos XVI–XX* (Mexico City: Fondo de Cultura Económica, 1990).

Kandell, Jonathan, *La Capital: The Biography of Mexico City* (New York: Random House, 1988).

Martínez, José Luis and Carballo, Emmanuel, *Lecturas de la Ciudad de México* (Mexico City: Consejo de la Crónica de la Ciudad de México, 1989).

Matos Moctezuma, Eduardo, *Tenochtitlan* (Mexico City: Fondo de Cultura Económica, 2006).

Quirarte, Vicente, *Elogio de la calle. Biografía literaria de la Ciudad de México (1850–1992)* (Mexico City: Ediciones Cal y Arena, 2001).

Soustelle, Jacques, *La vida cotidiana de los aztecas en vísperas de la conquista* (Mexico City: Fondo de Cultura Económica, 1983).

6. THE CINEMATIC CITY
A City Created by Film: Mexico City in Movies, 1977–2007

HUGO LARA CHÁVEZ

The highest building in Mexico City, the Torre Reforma, was built on the site of an old movie theatre, the Chapultepec, which, in turn, had been constructed within the grounds of cinema studios that had the same name. With the passing of time, we have forgotten how this location has been transformed. The changes might be seen as the natural transformation of urban spaces as a result of modernization, but they could also be viewed as an image of the dismantling of Mexican cinema in recent decades.

For those who love Mexico City, movies have become a kind of refuge that allows them to revisit old streets and old buildings, the attractions and the dramas of other times, other forms of coexistence and, even, other customs. But for young city dwellers, who have no other frame of reference except the chaotic and colourful environment that they are faced with each day, national cinema can be a way of discovering a marvellous city in perpetual motion, a vigorous city, both ancient and modern, which is being built every day.

Mexican cinema has been a great mirror of our city, its different areas and its significant moments in history, throughout the twentieth century and into this century. From the pioneers of early cinema right through to current directors, cinema has defined us both individually and collectively.

Almost since the inception of sound, national cinema, an urban art form, has repeatedly chosen Mexico City as both protagonist and backcloth. And in its journey through the urban landscape, its tenements and large mansions, its wide thoroughfares and narrow streets, Mexican cinema has missed nothing, however memorable or shameful, appealing, or disheartening. And in this play of contrasts, Mexico City has been the preferred setting and often the silent protagonist of dramas, passions, crimes, adventures and romance in every film genre in every period of history.

Keeping pace with the voracious growth of this city, Mexican cinema, like that of other cities across the world, has presented images and ideas that are both a portrait and an illusion. As it has developed, our national cinema has shaped this city as a component part of our identity and also as a witness to the transformations of this identity. Between the morally instructive brothels of *Santa* (Antonio Moreno, 1932) and the scatological images of *Santa sangre* (*Holy Blood*, Alejandro Jodorowsky, 1998) there are as many miles of asphalt, as there are between the avenues that lead from the shocking misery of *Los olvidados* (*The Forgotten Ones*, Luis Buñuel, 1950) to the urban horror of *El callejón de los milagros* (*Midaq Alley*, Jorge Fons, 1995).[1]

The last three decades

The focus of this chapter is a city created by cinema, but it could also be called a cinema created by the city, and it is this dynamic interplay, this two-way game, that I wish to explore. In this chapter I will focus on the last three decades, 1977–2007, a period in which some of the symbols and social expressions used to delineate the city have grown in strength, while others have been consolidated, to create Mexico City's current identity. In some cases these have been put onto film intentionally, in other cases they seem to appear through chance, filtered in a natural way, like a quiet stage that becomes alive in the rush of the streets, the buildings, the crowds or the sound of engines and markets.

During these thirty years, all the transformations of the city and its inhabitants, their emotions, their dreams and joys, have made their way to the screen. There's no doubt that the vigorous city has generated these expressions. The very nature of the Federal District, as the political, religious, economic and cultural centre of the country, seems to exceed all limits. It is a colossus that is impossible to define from just one point of view, a leviathan that cannot be captured in only one image, because as soon as this colossus lifts one of its limbs we have missed the perspective of the other. But perhaps, through the medium of film, we can get closer to that huge body, creating a faithful image of the whole and offering portraits of each of its parts. In this way the focused eye of the moving image becomes a most useful tool for visualizing an immeasurable wholeness.

That never-ending totality can be seen from different angles at crucial moments in the city's history. Take, for example *Lola*, María Novaro's feature from 1987. Here we see a city destroyed after the 1985 earthquake, with damaged buildings that work as background to emphasize the emotional drama of a young working-class mother who manages to survive in the middle of an economic crisis and the politics of a country impoverished by the old PRI regime. This woman's story is organically linked to the col-

---

[1] Only approved English-language titles to the movies have been included here.

Figure 6.1   *Lola* (1987). Still by Guadalupe Sánchez.

lective feeling of the city at that moment. Director María Novaro admirably portrays the desolation and pessimism of this environment.

But there's also the city that aspires to the cosmopolitan world promised by globalization in the early nineties in *Sólo con tu pareja* (*Love in the Time of Hysteria*, 1990), Alfonso Cuarón's first feature. The film tells of the fling between an advertising executive and a flight attendant, with the AIDS epidemic as a background. This comedy breathes the air of the 'new' Mexico announced by the presidency of Carlos Salinas (1988–94), with its Holy Trinity of the North America Free Trade Agreement (NAFTA), its cosmopolitan aspirations, and its exploration of a new popular culture free of complications and stress. Here the urban spaces, the Angel de La Independencia and the Torre Latinoamericana glisten in the luminous gaze of the cinematographer Emmanuel Lubezki, and would have us believe that we live in a city of hope. Cuarón also explores the other city, of intense contrasts, in *Y tu mamá también* (2001). Here he uses young protagonists from different social groups as a way of focusing on urban contradictions, at a moment when the modernization party seems to be over, when the

NAFTA agreement is seen to have failed, and new social actors appear, such as the Zapatista movement, demonstrating in the Paseo de la Reforma. An off-screen narrator points out the social contradictions of the moment as the boys in the film pursue their hedonistic love triangle.

Before continuing, it would be useful to ask ourselves if there is a film identity in Mexico City, among this mixture of diverse or even opposite images that shape the filmography of hundreds of films. Lacking an identifiable architecture such as New York or one of the many universal symbols we find in London or Paris, what are the elements that make up the cinema of Mexico City? What do totally different films such as *Temporada de patos* (*Duck Season*, 2004) by Fernado Eimbcke or *Amores perros* (*Love's a Bitch*, 2000) by Alejandro González Iñárritu have in common?

During these thirty years, we have been able to see a shared path of a cinema and a city that has left its splendour behind. A city that was facing new dilemmas and the need to find a link with its inhabitants and its public—with their new tastes, trends, and preferences—experienced changes that have had an influence on both films and the life of the city itself. Let me list some of these major areas: the struggle for democracy in the country; the transformation of streets into highways; the opening up of the city and the country to the dynamics of globalization; the importance of urban counter-cultures; the diversification of entertainment with cinema no longer the favourite form of entertainment for the masses; the transformation of neighbourhoods and their traditions; ideological diversification; the industrialization of crime; the support for the rights of women and minorities.

How can this complex spectrum be described other than through movies? Through cinema we can see these different aspects of the city: the contrasts, the resistance, the break-up, the changes, the indifference, the solitude. Mexico City has been both metaphor and reality of the contradictory nature of our country, of almost all classes, a codex than unfolds and describes maturity and precociousness, nobility and injustice, and development as well as chaos and corruption.

The horror of emptiness

Salvador Novo, one of the greatest chroniclers of Mexico City, defined its urban density as a reaction against the 'horror of emptiness', that is, the vital need for city bustle and the ways people get along in the daily crowd. One of the constants of Mexican cinema has been its location in the *vecindad* (the tenement buildings) and the *barrio* (the local neighbourhood). In films from the forties and fifties this idealized space was usually made up of the following characters: a hero, usually a poor but noble and hardworking

Figure 6.2 *El callejón de los milagros* (1995). Still by Federico García.

young man, a long suffering mother who prevented her children from going off the rails and of course villains, characters who are usually redeemed through remorse and a guilty conscience. *El callejón de los milagros*, directed by Jorge Fons, gives a modern inflection to the *vecindad* and the *barrio*, spaces in which the passions, dreams and frustrations of a group of characters intermingle. Here, the *vecindad* is depicted as the historical habitat of the city's inhabitants, especially those belonging to the popular classes. The movie is based on the novel by the Egyptian writer Naguib Mahfouz, and the drama is transferred to Mexico City with authenticity: the streets are full of shops and food stands, the houses are in ruins, and they shelter all kinds of characters, the dealers and the poets, the hookers and the bureaucrats. But in this modern version of the *vecindad* movie, all the dreams of the protagonists in the three interlocking stories are frustrated.

In the same tradition, Fernando Sariñana's movie *Ciudades oscuras* (*Dark Cities*, 2002), describes a series of crimes that take place in the downtown area in just one night. All the violent episodes are connected, as well as the victims and their killers. In Mexico City, crimes are also committed in big numbers.

In the eighties, the *barrio* was one of the favourite settings of Mexican cinema, featuring low-budget films produced for domestic distribution. These kinds of features usually starred comedians, and the characters they played were caught up in erotic adventures. The city and its neighbourhoods are an integral part of this cinema, in movies such as *La pulquería* (Víctor Manuel Castro, 1981), where its protagonists celebrate laughter, riotous living and promiscuity, as a form of escape from the social, political and economic stagnation in that period.

But there is another type of cinema that touches the raw nerves of urban reality and its intricate human geography. *El héroe* (*The Hero*, 1995) shows a darker side of this crowded world, this horror of emptiness, which is full of paradoxes. Luis Carlos Carrera's short film won the Golden Palm in Cannes in 1995. It is an animated movie about a man who tries to save a young woman from committing suicide in the underground. This ironic tale reveals the loneliness of a certain kind of life and shows that our actions are based on collective priorities.

The paradox of anonymity

Mexico City is inside an urban zone populated by over twenty million inhabitants, though officially only ten million belong to its Federal District. In these conditions, Mexico City inhabitants have learned that, in contrast to the discomforts of this crowded living space, anonymity can be both an advantage but also a predicament. The individuals of our urban cinema are normally anonymous characters, citizens from the streets, who have no influence either in history or on political or social change. But these characters are usually affected by the state of the nation and by external forces. They live out their intimate dramas, in their seemingly simple and peaceful daily lives, until a conflict erupts which immerses them in the external forces of their reality.

In *Todo el poder* (1998), filmmaker Fernando Sariñana looks to these kinds of characters, in the story about a publicist and an actress. Both of them tired of the insecurity and dangers of the city and of police inefficiency, they make a plan to capture the thieves who robbed them in a restaurant. Here the thirty or so upper middle-class protagonists aim to strike a blow against the 'express' robberies in bars and restaurants that were so much a feature of the time and, in so doing, they uncover sinister links between the thieves and the dishonest authorities. The movie is narrated as a comedy, and has a happy ending, a kind of small civil revenge on the screen against the system. It is a moment, of course, when the old political system of the PRI is in crisis, as would be seen by their defeat in the 2000 elections.

By contrast, Armando Casas's movie *Un mundo raro* (2001), examines the same topic from the point of view of a group of criminals who kidnap a famous TV personality. One of the abductors is a wannabe comedian, so he comes to an agreement with the kidnapped actor who offers him an opportunity to break into the world of show business. But, of course, the young man does not achieve this leap from the anonymous world of crime to the world of the television celebrity, since the media environment turns out to be as cruel, or even worse, than the life of crime.

A similar theme is explored in Luis Estrada's film *Un mundo maravilloso* (*A Wonderful World*, 2006). It once again examines the conflicts of an individual who survives in the anonymity of urban poverty. But it is his misfortune to be attracted by the lure of fame when a group of politicians use him to earn votes and charm the electorate. They turn him into the model citizen of a country governed by opportunists, who have announced with a great fanfare the country's new democratic freedoms and its status as a developed nation.

Anonymity in Mexico City is not productive when someone has to face up to the plots of history. Ordinary citizens are easily neutralized if they struggle against the injustice all around them. In a city where everything moves in masses, where everything is quantified in millions and where there can be a dozen demonstrations in the same day, individual struggles are usually relegated to the background, even if they represent legitimate causes.

Some of the most relevant movies in this regard have used the idea of placing ordinary people up against the power structures. These films are set at moments that have defined not only the city but the entire country, analysing individual dramas from a civil rights perspective. For instance, in the movie *Bandera rota* (*Broken Flag*, Gabriel Retes, 1977) a group of film students by accident capture on film the murder of a woman by her husband, a powerful businessman. But instead of turning him over to the police, they decide to blackmail him, their demands being that he offers better conditions for the workers in his factories. The young men are left-wing dreamers, from a generation influenced by the events of 1968 in Mexico. But the students fail to realize that the businessman has gained enormous popularity among the population for his various activities. Meanwhile, the young men are identified and then brutally dealt with. In a similar vein, the movie *Conejo en la luna* (*Rabbit on the Moon*, Jorge Ramírez Suàrez, 2004) focuses on ordinary citizens caught up by mistake in a political conspiracy. Here a man and his British wife meet a policeman, who is part of a conspiracy to murder a political figure.

A tragic outcome is inevitable for anonymous citizens who, by chance or deliberately, get sucked into the vortex of the main plot, because this is a space traditionally marked out for power groups. This painful fact is explored in Jorge Fons's film *Rojo amanecer* (*Red Dawn*, 1989), the first fictional film to narrate the true events of the 1968 repression. The film focuses on a family that lives in a modest apartment, just opposite the square, the Plaza de las Tres Culturas in Tlatelolco, where thousands of students are demonstrating against the government. They witness the brutal repression from their window, and this repression ends up encompassing them, when policemen looking for those who have escaped the massacre in the square enter their apartment and kill all the members of the family.

But fate is not the only mechanism at play between the anonymous individual and the historical moment, since often it is a question of making daily moral and ethical choices. By making these choices, these characters aim to transform the natural order of their lives. In Arturo Ripstein's movie *Cadena perpetua* (1978), the imprisoned protagonist's goal is to become an ordinary citizen, and not return to his criminal past, because he has found honest employment, as a bank teller, and has a family to support.

Figure 6.3 *Cadena perpetua* (1978). Still by Ángel Corona.

Los ladrones viejos. Las leyendas del artegio (2007) is the most recent movie by filmmaker Everardo González, a feature film where he portrays real life, legendary, old-fashioned thieves who steal without causing any damage and without leaving obvious traces. The most famous of them, 'El Carrizos', broke into the house of President Luis Echeverría, and stole everything he wanted, without being detected by the military escort that was protecting the building. He was unaware whose the house was, but when he found out he felt proud to have achieved this break-in.

When anonymous individuals try to change their destiny they face many invisible barriers, which stop them or punish them. In my city, this is not just a question of political positions, but also of atavistic social customs. In *Retrato de una mujer casada* (*A Married Woman*, Alberto Bojórquez, 1979), the protagonist, a married young woman with two children, fights for her personal aspirations, enrols at the university and looks for a space to develop as a person, but her husband and her own parents, spoil this dream. The anonymous individual must remain caught in her own narrow sphere.

The need for resistance

Resistance is a basic condition of life in Mexico City, not only in social or political terms, but in everyday life. It is not by chance that drama has been the genre most cultivated by our cinema. But this resistance to bitter reality works as a survival mechanism rather than anything more positive, a defence mechanism like caimans changing colour.

But the city and its cinema also express the paradoxes of life in this daily struggle for survival. Here we see how city dwellers have to solve their different problems, especially their personal battles: how to pay the mortgage, or how to educate their children, or how a couple can resolve difficulties in their relationship.

In Juan Antonio de la Riva's movie *Elisa antes del fin del mundo* (*Elisa Before the End of the World*, 1996), a ten-year-old girl suffers because the economic crisis—specifically the financial crash of 1994—has led to a breakdown in the relationship between her parents. Here the games and fantasies of the girl and her young friends are played out within an ever encroaching adult world of crisis. Elisa's fascination with cockroaches, for example, is a strange image of innocence and horror that seems to be a premonition of bad times to come. To try to alleviate the family situation, she turns her fantasy world into adult reality and plans to rob a bank, with tragic results.

The inhabitants of Mexico City have learned to live with their own paranoia, the neurosis of others and the dissent of everyone. They must try to find a delicate and fragile balance among these different concerns and, when this balance is lost, the unexpected can occur.

A detective who is a part of a group of corrupt policemen, has to spend time in jail to satisfy his superiors, but the plan is that he will be released in a short period of time and then return to join to the group. But in jail he is attacked by many criminals from whom he had extorted money or whom he had tortured in the past. The prisoners make him lose his mind. Nevertheless, he escapes and begins a crusade against crime, as a modern Don Quixote. This is the plot of Alfredo Gurrola's movie *Llámame Mike* (*Call Me Mike*, 1979). The policeman survives all these attacks and, ultimately, all his former cronies are astonished when he is honoured and granted freedom so that he can continue his crusade against criminals on the street. 'But . . . he's a madman', somebody says to the police chief, 'Madman?' he retorts, looking out of the window at the streets below. 'Have you seen this city?'

In discussions about Mexican cinema, there are those who criticize the fact that our city is always being portrayed from its ugly side, that misery and poverty predominates, not the beauty, or the comfort and luxury that is evident in the richer areas. There are those who feel offended because these films repeatedly show to the world the violent and aggressive city of Alejandro Gonzalez Iñárritu's *Amores perros*, or the street children who survive abandoned in the city, as in Gerardo Tort's first movie, *De la calle* (*Streeters*, 2001). But can movies avoid this, ignore this unhappy reality that exists and is so very visible?

It is true that this is not the only possible subject matter. There are also the cosmopolitan city conflicts, in movies such as Antonio Serrano's *Sexo, pudor y lágrimas* (*Sex, Shame and Tears*, 1998), a tale about the dissatisfaction of several young couples when faced with the emptiness of their existence. Set in the cosmopolitan area of Polanco and in the richly appointed flats of these university-trained, middle-class characters, the emotional triangles of the three couples explore areas of infidelity, frustration, insecurity and self betrayal.

Enrique Begne's film *Dos abrazos* (*Two Embraces*, 2007) tells two stories. The first is rooted in the reality of the middle class, who are seen as survivors, coping with the contradictory desires for independence and also for affection, love and friendship. This is narrated through the story of a supermarket cashier and a teenager who create a loving relationship, in the midst of their dislocated family lives. The second story focuses on a taxi driver, whose passenger falls into a coma. Through this, he meets the passenger's daughter, with whom he begins an intimate relationship, which becomes one between two people caught up in the uncertainties of life.

Figure 6.4
Amores perros
(2000). Still by
Federico
García.

Figure 6.5 *Sexo, pudor y lágrimas* (1998). Still by Daniel Daza.

To resist the city, that urban and aggressive reality, it is necessary to be anchored by an illusion, by the possibility of aspiring to something; preferably love. The inhabitants of the city depend on such illusions in order to face up to daily life. In Jaime Humberto Hermosillo's film *Naufragio* (1978), an old woman who is tired of city life lives obsessed with the thought that her only son will one day return. He had left home years ago to travel and seek adventure. Her idolatry is shared by a girl who rents a room in her apartment. Both women construct an illusion based on nothing, in the middle of their routine, humdrum lives, but they manage to survive thanks to the dream they share. But when this dream appears alive, it turns out that their illusion is shattered.

In Arturo Ripstein's *Principio y fin* (*The Beginning and the End*, 1993), based on another novel of Naguib Mahfouz, a woman who has been widowed, decides to invest all the family efforts for the benefit of her spoiled youngest son. She forces her three elder sons to sacrifice themselves for this goal. In this world, the worst threat seems to come from the intimacy of the family, the root of our lives and of our frustrations and demons. Seen from the outside, this asphyxiating world of the home is an illusion that we should mistrust. The cinema of the city has certain weakness for portraying such family tragedies, through which we can uncover the complex texture of society, its loyalties and phobias.

Figure 6.6 *Principio y fin* (1993). Still by Federico García.

A place of contrasts

The great contrasts to be found in Mexico City are outlined in *Batalla en el cielo* (*Battle in Heaven*, 2005). Here it seems that director Carlos Reygadas has set out with the clear intention of irritating and even offending his audience. The film's subversive, provocative charge has made it famous in a very short period of time. Yet it is a curious fact that while its images seem to come from a twisted, febrile imagination, they have obvious links with many other films and with our own chaotic reality. It traces the development of a killer between two crimes, one involuntary and the other premeditated.

Marcos, the wretched protagonist, and his wife are involved in the kidnap and death of a baby. Overcome with remorse, Marcos confesses his crime to his boss, Ana, a rich young woman, the daughter of a high-ranking military officer, and he begins a sexual relationship with her. The many contrasts here, between rich and poor, the beauty of the body of the young woman and the obese naked body of Marcos, the twisted morality of the protagonist, are all set within the horizons of the city. Here the city is a massive grey dot whose characters change colour with the environment. Usually the air is full of smoke or pollution which blot out, except for a few days in the year, the mountains and volcanoes that surround the city.

Figure 6.7 *Batalla en el cielo* (2005). Courtesy Fernanda Romandía.

Nicolás Echeverría's romantic comedy *Vivir mata* (*Living Kills*, 2001) offers a tour around the historic locations of the city and the many amazingly varied and disparate sites and locations. Some of these settings—in particular the La Merced district in the Centro Histórico of the city—are also shown by Alejandro Jodorowsky in *Santa Sangre* (*Holy Blood*, 1989). This area allowed Jodorowsky to compose his surreal fantasy around the contrasts to be found in poverty between despair and love, misery and compassion. The director melds fantasy and reality: just as the blue and red spirals usually represent the human DNA structure, *Santa Sangre* is founded on the spirals of the reality and the madness of Mexico City.

The cityscape, perhaps, can be the site of redemptive magic. This is one of the premises of the film *El mago* (*The Magician*, 2004), about a street magician who feels the need to pay his debts to the past when he is diagnosed with a terminal brain tumour. Instead of being stricken by hopelessness, the character goes out bravely to confront what is left of his life. The director Jaime Aparicio offers an authentic urban fable, with neighbourhood heroes and princesses—the film is set in a rundown, violent environment, with prostitutes and drug dealers and decaying tenements—with villains who endanger the lives of innocent people, all of whom require the intervention of our magician, Tadeo, the defender of noble causes.

Magic and misery are images used to describe our urban landscape. In the cinema, such magic can sometimes be a way of warding off tragedy or an escape from harsh realities. Dana Rotberg's movie *Angel de fuego* (*Angel of Fire*, 1991) looks at the oppressive life of a teenager who is employed in a circus and who lives through misery and marginality, misogyny and domestic violence. The characters of our urban cinema look always for the magic formula against unhappiness, an antidote that allows them some relief from their distress. This formula sometimes comes in the form of a fragrance, as happens in Marisa Sistach's film *Perfume de violeta. Nadie te oye* (*Violet Perfume: Nobody Hears You*, 2000). It brings about the friendship of two teenagers even though their personalities are very different. The fragrance of violets becomes the symbol of this possible happiness amongst hardship and poverty. Sistach offers an unadorned picture of city life in working-class neighbourhoods, a vision portrayed in simple and extremely effective language. We are offered a view of public places such as the market, the city buses or the secondary schools, where rule breaking is a form of survival.

A moment of magic can assuage desperation and misery, but perhaps the most current outlook in many contemporary movies is the discouraging view that it is impossible to change one's fate: 'If you want to make God laugh, tell him your plans', says one of the characters in *Amores perros*.

The valley of surprises

The inhabitants of Mexico City and the characters in urban cinema can lead their lives in the midst of surprises, or, rather, they are adept at incorporating unusual things into their routine. Of course they can do this in a place where public buses compete in speed trials with super expensive cars, or where paper houses exist side by side with ultramodern office buildings. Almost all the urban movies try to exploit this raw material, the unusual element in the stories of common people.

Unemployed workers form a line outside the city cathedral, where they put an advertisement to offer their services as plumbers, masons or carpenters, while inside the church, the priest prays for the richest businessman of the country. In *El Milusos* (Roberto G. Rivera, 1980), we are told the story of a peasant who comes to the city in search of work and better opportunities but ends up beaten and humiliated until he finds himself in jail. There, he manages to join the community in such a way that he finds that life in jail offers him a more prosperous life. Unfortunately for him, he is set free and thrown out on the streets once more.

A photographer is struck in a political meeting which is broken up by the police and paramilitary groups in 1971, and stays in coma for twenty years. This is the basis of *El bulto* (Gabriel Retes, 1991), about a character who wakes up and is surprised by a new reality. The country is joining the globalized world and his former friends and relatives, former leftist militants, have given up their ideological principles: 'Look at you! You look like aristocrats!' the protagonist says reproachfully to his sister and brother-in-law, ex-hippies like him. 'Great!', she replies proudly.

People in Mexico City inhabit a place and a country which sometimes seems the opposite of logical. The city itself begins in this way. It was raised on four lakes that little by little have been drying up and the city sinking with it, literally. It cannot be a surprise that we now are living through a crisis in our water supply. Neither is it a surprise for our citizens to find that the authorities who deny responsibility for such crises have their pockets full of money, or that they reject accusations for violent events with blood on their hands, or that the richest businessman in the world comes from a place immersed in poverty.

Our city and its movies have always been associated with absurdities and surprises. The city is the stage for our fears and hopes, amidst walls and barriers, which can be visible or invisible. Simón Bross's movie *Malos hábitos* (*Bad Habits*, 2007) is one such labyrinth. It tells the story of a rich anorexic woman, who tortures her nine-year-old daughter so that she will lose weight. There is also a nun who performs strange acts of penance with food offerings. Obviously these incidents themselves are surprising. But what is equally surprising is that these lonely characters suffer almost in silence, and that the people they live with do not recognize the gravity of their situation.

In our city and in our cinema, there is always a surprise element, something that escapes any plan and that upsets the calculations of the experts. Who would have thought, for example—taking examples from recent years—that a Mexican film would enjoy greater box office success than a Hollywood blockbuster; that one of our filmmakers would have a major influence on cinema throughout the world; that an actor and a cinematographer would achieve international success after honing their talents in our movie world with its limited resources; that the viewing public would flock to see Mexican movies? None of these was expected, and perhaps this element of the unsuspected or unforeseen is what determines the development of the city and our cinema, for better or worse. Both are currently being built without control in this valley of surprises.

Further Reading

Aviña, Rafael and Susana Casarín, *Una familia de tantas: una visión del cine social en México* (Mexico City: Sedesol, Conaculta, Imcine, 2000).

Ayala Blanco, Jorge, *La condición del cine mexicano* (Mexico City: Posada, 1986).

———, *La disolvencia del cine mexicano* (Mexico City: Grijalbo, 1991).

———, *La eficacia del cine mexicano* (Mexico City: Grijalbo, 1996).

———, *La fugacidad del cine mexicano* (Mexico City: Océano, 2001).

———, *La grandeza del cine mexicano* (Mexico City: Océano, 2004).

De la Vega Alfaro, Eduardo, ed., *Microhistorias del cine en México* (Mexico City: Universidad de Guadalajara, UNAM, IMCINE, Cineteca Nacional and Instituto Mora, 2006).

Hershfield, Joanna and David Maciel, eds, *Mexico's Cinema: A Century of Film and Filmmaking* (Wilmington, DE: Scholarly Resources, 1999).

Lara Chávez, Hugo, *Una ciudad inventada por el cine* (Mexico City: Cineteca Nacional, 2006).

Paranaguá, Paulo Antonio, ed., *Mexican Cinema* (London: BFI/IMCINE, London, 1995).

7. THE PHOTOGRAPHIC CITY
A City Heading in the Opposite Direction
MAGALI TERCERO

I. Introduction

A population of over twenty million people, sixteen boroughs (or delegaciones), with 70 per cent of the inhabitants on a low income, have formed a society that, for more than forty years now, has been leaving home in search of the American Dream. In 1996 photographer Maya Goded and I worked on a feature about prostitution in the La Merced district, in downtown Mexico City—what has recently been called the Centro Histórico or Historic Centre of the city. What we saw was a great deal of poverty and misery in the little bedrooms where the prostitutes took their clients, misery in the clothes of the men who paid for what for a few years now has been called the sex industry, and misery in the emotional lives of the protagonists. In those days Goded was a kind of Virgil who introduced me to those women in Manzanares Street who, at noon, crossed the street so that they could be chosen. It was through her that I met a thirty-five-year-old woman, very slim and quite a joker; a L'Oréal blonde who walked aided by a rudimentary pair of crutches because, in her childhood, she had suffered from poliomyelitis. She lived from prostitution since, apart from not being unattractive, she was very intelligent and was always willing to listen to the sorrows of others. Perhaps that is why this chapter is entitled 'A City Heading in the Opposite Direction', because many of the people interviewed survive while being openly marginalized by their country. Here I offer a number of chronicles of city life taken from my book, Cien freeways, *portraits of an intensely complex city that constantly evades the grasp of those who describe it in writing, through photographs or in films. The first is taken from 2005.*

'This is a farce, isn't it?' exclaims the taxi driver, a sturdy man who must be more than sixty-five, sporting a white-haired ponytail that I find quite ridiculous. Someone on the radio repeatedly mentions René Bejarano. Fed up, my interlocutor reaches out and turns the chatter off. In April the magazine *Letras Libres* created a polemic by proposing that the current media Babel should be organized with a series of debates broadcast on television and radio.

In the art fair I found a Portuguese magazine, *W Art*. An apt quotation caught my eye: 'The fact that people feel the need to hear the news several times a day is in itself a sign of anguish.' I am following this train of thought when the taxi driver shows me a resident's card issued in Georgia, in the United States. 'I went there in 1979, to try to improve my finances, and now that I've retired from lorry driving, I'm coming back.' He hasn't done badly: he has three taxis in Mexico, and drives one of them when he comes to visit; his children and grandchildren are doing quite well in Georgia; they managed to buy a house in both countries, have lived in comfort and the second generation went to college. But he wants to come back to the homeland. 'People tell me I'm mad. Tell me honestly, how do you find DF?[1] Because I will come back, no matter what.'

I delay my answer a bit because I have seen on repeated occasions how, against all the odds, people do go back to their country. In the end I tell him: 'You'll most likely end up returning to Georgia; you won't be able to fit back into DF, but you need to find out for yourself; there's no other way', I declare sententiously. Halfway down the arterial road we are over-taken by a silent police van driving at full speed in the opposite direction, down the bus lane. The taxi driver gets upset. 'Please don't be offended, but . . . you know what I think of Mexico? I think that our worst vice is indolence. It's a kind of disease. That's why we lack knowledge, technology. People don't work more than they have to, and they do that badly. Don't take offence, OK?'

And I don't. He's right. 'It's sad', we both say in unison. The downpour intensifies. I cry, you cry, we cry. I took the taxi as I left an Afro-Cuban dance lesson given by a writer from the island. What surprises me today, apart from all those complex steps of the *guaguancó*, is that I like—I love— the gravity of the Cuban instructor as he goes about his work. The guy in the taxi would shower him with praise, but discipline is not enough to build a great country. The worst thing of all is the widespread unwilling-ness to look at oneself in the mirror. Isn't that a more serious ill than indolence?

II. *A night with prostitutes*

The issue of prostitution is fascinating in itself, but I feel that we women can approach it from a different perspective. Maya Goded's photographs, like this one that shows a girl having a tattoo done, with the word dream appearing like a talisman,

[1] From 'Distrito Federal', meaning Mexico City.

Figure 7.1 Prostitute, Mexico City, 1999. © Maya Goded.

offer a view of women's reality that is both indignant and compassionate. Many years ago a photographer friend of mine, born in England, told me that in DF women are not treated like people. Perhaps that is why prostitution is impossible to prevent. I think it epitomizes the low esteem in which women are held. This excerpt from 1990 may give you an idea of what it means to be a prostitute in Mexico City.

A few months ago two American friends—a journalist and a photographer—came to DF to do a feature on prostitution in Mexico. An image from their account stayed with me: the moment when the photographer was left alone with one of the women. 'When I stroked her breasts there was milk', he said, 'and when I touched her sex she was bleeding. She had just given birth five days earlier. She insisted on telling me that she didn't have her period and offered to have sex with me. I couldn't go on. It was terrible.' Gaby, the most articulate of the prostitutes I interviewed tonight, says that she kept on working up to the seventh month of her second pregnancy (she has three children). 'Around that time my mother divorced my stepfather and went to San Luis Potosí. To be honest, I didn't care about my child's father; I had been living with him for a year, I even supported him, and when I told him about the pregnancy he took all my stuff and left me stranded in the hotel with a 135,000 peso bill; I was three months pregnant. I left the hotel and went to live with my brother, but he didn't agree with me working while I was pregnant. One of the owners of the place told me: "I'll send you to a doctor!", so I went to the surgery and the doctor was out of his head, drunk and on coke, so I said to myself, "No way! I won't have the operation!" There was no problem working like that; it used to turn some boys on. Now I'm sterilized, but before that I tried to avoid pregnancy with injections and pills, and in spite of that I got pregnant twice.'

III. Zapatistas in the Zócalo

Social struggles usually start when poverty begins to choke people. That was the case in the early twentieth century, during the revolutionary period. The original Zapatistas fought at that time, and their postmodern namesakes took up a similar struggle at the end of the twentieth century. I wrote this chronicle in 2001, when Subcomandante Marcos reached the Zócalo in Mexico City.

By chance we find ourselves on the balcony of room 606 in the Majestic Hotel, standing by Rosario Robles,[2] who today appears dressed in shocking-pink (what in our country we call '*Rosa Mexicano*'; literally, Mexican Pink). Below us we can see countless coloured dots: the crowd that moves in waves across the expanse of the city's main square; the flag flutters vigorously against the magnificent blue sky this 12th of March. The Zapatistas are already standing on the dais and seem to me to have too many clothes on in the intense heat. The sound system is awful. We can see the Cathedral, the National Palace, Madero and 20 de Noviembre Avenues, but we can't hear a thing. Rosario Robles admits how moved she has been by the people. And Mariana, her seventeen-year-old daughter, shares this

---

[2] A former head of government of Mexico City.

feeling. This is not just another day for anyone present, either up here or down there in the throng. Beyond ideologies, beyond being extreme blue, yellow, black, green, red or white,[3] passions have been unleashed here. On our way to the Zócalo, the taxi driver of the ecological Volkswagen was furious. This was the day the Zapatistas ended their twelve-day journey in convoy that had started in the depths of Chiapas and would be rounded off on 26 March with a speech by an indigenous woman, Commander Esther, addressed to the Mexican Congress, marking a rather extraordinary renewal of the peace dialogue. 'What the hell has Marcos been doing for seven years, hiding away there in the jungle?' asks our grumpy driver over and over again. Later on I ask Rosario Robles the same question. She answers quickly with a smile, brushing aside the taxi driver's criticism: 'Hitting a raw nerve. That's all.'

There are so many strong emotions. There are those—for example, the ice-lolly sellers—who wonder whether Marcos wants to see the Indians of Mexico stuck in reservations as in the United States. We mention this to one of the convoy's Huichol coordinators, who reacts with dignity: 'I have more important things on my mind than the remarks of ignorant people.' Then there is the anthropologist who, after harbouring many doubts about Marcos—who now competes with Vicente Fox for the covers of weekly journals, both riding their respective horses—has decided to talk to him. She has managed to do so and now she says that all her doubts have been cleared up and that she admires the man behind the subcomandante's myth, a myth that he himself—according to what he told veteran journalist Julio Scherer—didn't anticipate would grow to this extent. There are of course men who quietly laugh at the sight of women 'in love' with Marcos, as if they themselves had not written gushing articles about Gloria Trevi or other stars. And there are also those who irately declaim that *zapatismo* 'defends only a particular group of Indians'. 'What about the Indians in the north of the country?' asks a woman who lived for six years in Miami and has recently come back to Mexico. Marcos has been the object of all sorts of comments since 1 January 1994; first there was the speculation as to whether his movement was financed by the PRI in order to destabilize the country, and now the claims are that he has sold out to the PAN or that he's been corrupted and has accepted that foreigners should come and exploit our natural resources. This is gossip time, then, airing our likes and dislikes. The thing is, the matter at hand is serious. 'Mexico is plunged into confusion', the political analyst Samuel Schmidt emailed me from El Paso. Indeed, the only thing that's real this Sunday are the 250,000 people who

---

[3] A reference to the different colours by which followers of political parties or adherents to a particular political tendency are identified.

have put up with the intense sun just to hear Marcos talk, while Fox declares in some conference or other that 'we have to open up the Mexican market'.

There are also those who have not realized that this is not the seventies anymore, that the Cleta[4] performers and their old-fashioned shows, with all that '*folklorito* will never be defeated' paraphernalia, bore us to death in the cybernetic age, even if they are part of an economic reality. *How much? How much?* is the motto of our times. Or at least that's what it seems to be, because in Xochimilco, Subcomandante Marcos talked about the colour of money and the colour of the earth as opposed entities. There are even those, such as Félix, a peasant in his fifties from Milpa Alta, who says that he's willing to take up arms if there's no justice done to alleviate the misery of indigenous people.

IV. A day at the morgue

Another critical issue in Mexico City, also related to poverty, is the anonymous deaths of those who live on the streets and have no one to claim their bodies. This image shows a recently deceased man with no other company than a small crucifix hanging from the white wall.

Death—that frightens us all. But some deaths are more traumatic than others. For instance, those faced everyday by the doctors and medical students at the Forensic Medical Service (SEMEFO are the initials in Spanish). Every day, the bodies of people who have been murdered, committed suicide or have been killed in one of those barbaric accidents that happen everywhere, when a gun that someone's been playing with goes off, come to their premises in the Doctores neighbourhood. The staff of this institution, whose reports are checked against witness statements, seem to be used to the smell of death that impregnates the corridors of the small building. But someone like me, walking in off the street one day, just another reporter from the great metropolis, might want to run off and never come back to this place. The walls seem to be stained with the despair of relatives who have come here to look for the body of a loved one.

At the SEMEFO, around 7,000 post-mortems are performed every year, which, divided into the 365 days of the year, gives an average of eighteen or nineteen post-mortems a day. (Some are famous, like those of Polo Uscanga and Luis Miguel Moreno). The 'busiest' days are Fridays,

---

4 Popular and social theatre and culture organization with its origins in the 1970s.

Figure 7.2   Morgue, Mexico City, 2003. © Maya Goded.

Saturdays and Sundays, when the city's passions reach their extremes, along with public holidays.

In this place, and in some hospitals where post-mortems are performed, not all the dead are lucky enough to have an identity. According to Doctor Rodolfo Urquieta, SEMEFO's technical deputy director, every year there are 365 'unknowns'; 'as many as the days of the year'. Some of them are never claimed. And it is their photographs, along with an index card, that those who come looking for a missing relative must scrutinize every morning. Not everybody is photogenic, of course, but what we see here at the archives, in the first floor office, is the monstrous face of death. These

127

people—who were run over (*crushed* is the technical term), killed deliberately or accidentally, or committed suicide—these individuals, in their deep sleep of death, have not only suffered an undignified death but have also been subjected to a full and hurried post-mortem: they've had to be inspected front and back and then stitched up again, just like that. This whole procedure produces a weird broadening of the features, involuntary fierce expressions, malign imitations of humanity. Some of the bereaved come here to identify their relatives, but in fact the best proof of identity is the digital print of an injured finger, and so there is a strange archive of fingerprints that relatives can consult as a last resort. Unfortunately many of these dead never had, or have lost, documents such as their voting or military service card. For instance, the young men murdered in the Buenos Aires quarter were brought here, and we saw that their relatives had to have blood tests done in order to identify them.

As I write these words, the tape recorder clearly reproduces the sound of the instrument that is diligently cutting the dead man's skull in two, a lugubrious musical background to Dr Urquieta's commentary. In any other context the screech would be tolerable—at the time I tried to smother it by raising my voice. Now, as I transcribe the interview, unable to take refuge in amnesia, it's impossible to shut out the image of the man whose brains were blown out by a single shot (the Attorney General's office has declared that an accident was the probable cause of death). It is impossible not to bring to mind the gory mass slowly seeping from the skull and falling into a bucket positioned beside the stretcher. I turn the machine off with a sort of intense shudder and remember that I'd decided not to make a detailed description of the perpetual Day of the Dead in this cold building on Niños Héroes Avenue.

V. Who can stop a cruel mother?

Poverty and destitution are fundamental to issues such as the mistreatment of minors. The chronicle is both a journalistic and a literary genre that allows us to approach harsh, though perhaps not very visible, realities such as this, from a different perspective. Maya Goded's image is eloquent and subtle because in it there's a child who is hiding his pain and hoping to be rescued.

This taxi driver was special. In half an hour he gave an emphatic analysis of his last passenger's behaviour. 'She's cruel', he declared. He was referring to the violent behaviour of a forty-something woman. 'She had two children with her, and was yelling at the eldest: "You're not going to the movies! You're as stupid as your father. I always used to get top marks!"'

Figure 7.3 Mistreated child, Mexico City, 1997. © Maya Goded.

The driver caught my eyes in the rear-view mirror and saw my look of astonishment, not at the mother's abusive behaviour. No, I was surprised at his psychological perspicacity, his passionate defence of the anonymous child. 'She was also humiliating him, comparing him to his little brother.' Without waiting for an answer, he started to imitate the woman: 'Jorgito on the other hand . . . He really does love me', he mimicked in a falsetto voice. 'He's in the first grade of high school', continued the driver. 'He's at a difficult age. But she doesn't care', he added raising his voice. That's when I noticed he couldn't be more than twenty-seven. I told him that on 6 July 1997 millions of Mexican children had voted for their rights. According to the Federal Electoral Institute, 501,682 kids voted for 'stopping anyone from hurting my body and my feelings', and 499,959 voted for 'living in a peaceful place with people who look after me and always love me'. He liked the idea, but still retorted: 'Who's going to stop a cruel mother? Are they going to put her in jail because she calls her son an idiot?' I told him, as a joke, that I would have voted to have my mother arrested. He ignored me. 'That boy will end up a drug addict; there has to be a punishment for such parents.' I informed him as best as I could, because he didn't stop talking, that in 2003 there were already 3.5 million children working in Mexico, 170,000 living in the streets of the 100 main cities in our country, and 16,000 children sexually exploited every year. Fortunately, in recent years twenty-six states have passed legislation to prevent violence against 32.4 million minors.

I shouldn't have opened my mouth. He was all wound up again. 'But that's what is o-b-v-i-o-u-s. This woman's abuse isn't covered by the law.' He was absolutely right. I limited myself to a brief: 'Frustrated grown-ups do a lot of harm.' Then I read his particulars on his registration card: Roberto, born in 1977. I remember that year well. That's when I found out, dumbfounded, that my best friend felt extraordinarily free when her mother died. Later, she was ridden with guilt. Roberto was still utterly outraged: 'You don't even need to beat them up!' How can you control something as subtle as emotional mistreatment, the manipulation of love through a Pavlovian approach? In the United States children have a right to complain to the police about the insults—big or small—that they get from their parents. And they are heard!'

I thought that once again the taxi driver was right. The website 'Derechos sin infancia' ('Rights without childhood') states that the Law for the Protection of Children and Teenagers' Rights, passed in 2001 hasn't brought about any meaningful change in Mexico. Even worse, the UN's Children's Rights Committee's recommendations to the Mexican govern-ment have not been heeded. They also publish the goals of a campaign organized by the Red por los Derechos de la Infancia en México or Network for Children's Rights in Mexico. It is called: 'It's not enough that they are there. They have to be implemented.'

'She was damaging the younger child as well', continued the taxi driver, immersed in his indignant thoughts. 'Who?' I asked, putting aside the strange memories his conversation had brought up. 'The little smartass. I was so angry when he backed his mum . . .! The woman made the older child move so that the little pain-in-the-neck could sit in the middle! She told him: "Keep away from me or else . . .".' Then he went on to describe the passenger. 'She's very bitter. You can see it in her body language. I was about to tell her: "Careful; children grow up and have to face the world. Love your child if you don't want an enemy."' Now that touched me.

From the back seat I said he was right, that a psychotherapist I interviewed recently told me that feelings of shame are acquired between the first six months and two years of life. 'Shame at what?' he asked, gently making fun of me. I could not explain. Only professionals understand such subtle concepts, I thought. Or rather they make them up as an antidote against despair. Or in order to earn money. The taxi driver returned to the attack. 'There are even worse mothers', he said, with a trace of sadness in his voice. 'Yours, for instance?' I was about to ask, but he continued: 'A few days ago I had another passenger, very pretty, around twenty-six years old. She came running towards the car with a little boy. She was pulling him by his wrist like this. Then she slapped him. "Do you see why I'm always late for work?"' Roberto frowned. 'I felt like turning round and slapping her.'

By now we had reached Gutenberg Street. 'She didn't conceive that child with love', he declared quite convinced. Though, now that I think about it, the psychologist who talked about shame told me that there's a lot of love–hate in families, and that these things are passed down from one generation to the next. Isn't there any hope? Finally the driver asked me my name. 'Nice meeting you. I'm Roberto', he said, shaking my hand and attempting to kiss me goodbye, like a new friend. I was surprised. I bid him farewell from a distance. 'Say something to those mothers, please!' I shouted at him, but the car had already left.

VI. *There is no forgiveness. Tepepan Women's Prison*

Here I deal with the incredible range of emotions that I felt during a three-hour visit to the Tepepan Women's Prison. Although this chronicle about that women's jail dates from 1993, it could have been written yesterday.

Elvira's eyes light up when someone praises her hair. 'What do you do to it?' asks one of the inmates at the Tepepan Women's Prison. 'It looks so pretty!' She answers, cheerfully, that every Saturday she puts mayonnaise on her hair and one hour later rinses it with lots of water. Two seconds later her eyes are full of tears. I think that perhaps she remembered her Saturdays before prison, when her four children were still alive and she had not been sentenced to twenty-eight years in prison for filicide. Suddenly I can see again the four little white crosses driven into the earth floor of the asbestos and corrugated iron hut where Elvira, then twenty-three years old, lived with her children in 1983. The image froze me when the Lomas de Padierna residents took me to the scene of the crime. The people who live in that neighbourhood, which is unpaved and has no electricity or sewerage, are divided into two camps, for and against Elvira. Living in a small town can certainly be hell. Some of the people who condemn her would be happy to stone her. Or wouldn't we all? The judge, who was pregnant when the case was started, condemned her. Did I? At dawn on the day before the interview I woke up screaming: 'Put her away, lock her up and throw away the key, for the rest of her life!' It came straight from the heart. And just now I don't know if I should write this, because I can already see the look of horror in the eyes of the feminist psychologist Concepción Fernández. She has given Elvira therapeutic care since the murder and for five years she also paid lawyers, finding money where there was none to be found, in an attempt to keep the defendant out of prison, because she did not think she was guilty.

The person who is laughing most heartily is a portly green-eyed woman from Mazatlán. She must be around thirty-six years old, with very short brown hair. She's wearing men's clothes: grey suit trousers and a blue shirt over a white vest. Her name is Angélica Cuevas, and she's sentenced to twenty-five years for being the mastermind behind the murder of an old woman. 'Tell me, what did the woman do to you?', I ask. 'I mean, so that you wanted to kill her.' My indiscretion and the roar of laughter it provokes surprise everyone. Angélica then turns very serious and answers: 'Oh dear! It's a very long story! You can kill for many reasons. Out of despair, for instance. There were two of us accused, but since I was the pushy one—I'm a civil engineer—I ended up as the mastermind.' I sense her reticence and I decide to ask her to tell me instead what her plans are for when she's released. 'There's too much to do outside. I have my mother and two children. I won't be able to go back to my career because now I'm quite behind.' Beside her is her girlfriend Rubiela López, a blonde Colombian, strong as her, imprisoned for drug trafficking. 'Give me a break! It was just a few little pills!', she comments in pure Mexican slang. We laugh again and everyone's suddenly in a festive mood.

'Is being a drug trafficker what you really need?'

It's lunchtime and in the canteen everyone's in good humour. 'Hey, girl! What did you cook today?', asks a mulatta girl wearing a shocking-pink top and white jeans, her cry as rhythmic as a *cumbia*. 'Mmmm, stuffed chillies', she says when she sees the plate full of chillies and red rice. 'It's party time', shouts the girl humming a *cumbia* and dancing a few jaunty steps. Beside her, a beautiful woman in her thirties tries to smile. 'Come on, cheer up', says Fredesvinda, 'Next time they'll allow you your visit, you'll see.' The other answers: 'It's really fucked-up; everything here's an obstacle, and you're on your own.' Later on I'll find out that she's a prostitute and was caught with cocaine in Mazatlán. She's doing her sentence at the Reclusorio Norte (North Prison), but they brought her to Tepepan so that she can have psychological counselling. The gossip of the day is that two inmates swapped their secret conjugal visits. 'It's just that the other guy likes me more', she says knowingly.

'Hi there, I'm here for lunch!' pipes up a girl who seems to be strangely gentle in this place. Her long hair is dyed a light blond and done in a punk style. She's wearing a long T-shirt, leggings and tennis shoes. Her left arm is bent, motionless, against her side. Her name is Rocío Trejo, she's twenty-eight years old, charged with cocaine trafficking and sentenced to ten years. 'They tortured me at the PGR (the Attorney General's office)', she tells me showing me her arm. She's lost all feeling in the arm since the nerves were irreversibly damaged by the beatings she received for nine days at the PGR, two years ago. She shows me her legs, covered with cigarette burns.

'They tortured me and raped me. I saw a man, who was detained with me, die', Rocío starts her account in a neutral, even childlike voice. 'During the first eight days I refused to sign a false statement, though they were beating me up and raping me all the time. They had us on the floor, hands and feet manacled. They beat us with a metal rod. When they killed that man I told them that I would sign. First I wanted to kill myself but I couldn't because I didn't find anything to stab myself with. When they saw the corpse they brought me over here, because they didn't want problems.'

'One of my mates at the PGR was Sofía Anaya, the one who was with Zorrilla and who was involved in the Buendía murder. That woman was a cop and knew the law inside out. She had a really hard time! I took her to court as a witness for my defence. And she made a statement that I'd been beaten up, but they didn't listen. It makes you sick, you can't get anywhere', she says, tensing her face muscles almost imperceptibly. 'They sentenced me at around ten o'clock in the evening, and that was the time my judge was up for promotion. Around a month ago Dr Carpizo[5] gave his report on Human Rights and God knows what other goodies he was boasting about. I had to laugh, because none of it was true. Show me . . . where is my 640 file? When they come and see some of us in here and they show us some fair treatment, then Mr Carpizo can talk about his report. How is it possible that they've locked up a woman here for stealing a bottle of milk and a piece of cake?'

[5] Former Human Right's Ombudsman.

VII. *Five close-ups of* lucha libre *(masked wrestling)*

Let me now turn to lucha libre, *the sporting spectacle that lifts Mexicans out of their daily lives.*

Leaning over the head of his opponent, who is lying at his feet, El Negro Cuéllar—long black hair, naked torso and white shorts—buries his teeth into El Apache's left temple. Dozens of hypnotized eyes follow the action. Mouths gape and emit a muffled scream. Throwing back his hair with a vigorous movement of his neck, the wrestler spits upwards a jet of blood that soars briefly in the air. I concentrate on him and one image stands out: the tense male body, the chest arched backwards, the arms outstretched as if in greeting, the legs half bent in an open stance, the smooth chest, the neck leaning back and the wavy hair falling down his back. This body's stance is imperious. 'Wrestlers are like gods', Doña Virginia, the most passionate of *lucha libre's* fans remarked; she has an altar in her house to honour her earthly gods: *Máscara Sagrada* (The Sacred Mask), The Son of Santo, *Los Ángeles Blancos* (The White Angels). 'Let him go, fucking rat-tails!', shouts a furious woman behind me. 'They're like dogs. That's not wrestling, that's street fighting!', yells a younger woman at the top of her voice. For the sixth time, El Negro Cuéllar bites his rival viciously, and for the sixth time he throws back his head and shoulders elegantly and spits out a profuse jet of blood. I think of Dante, of the frozen sea where a sinner is for ever gnawing at the skull of a man who in life was his worst enemy. A child sings softly: 'The jet in the fountain became big, then became small.'[6]

This blood is very strange. Oddly clear and dense. 'Is it paint?' asks Rocío beside me. 'It's blood', comes the curt retort of a woman who was shouting her head off a moment ago. 'Well . . . It's a bit of blood and a bit of paint', observes her husband. 'The most common things here are the face bites and wounds', says Dr Esteban Núñez de Cáceres, the staff doctor at the Revolución Arena. 'Once we had to stop a bout with Pirate Morgan because of a very serious haemorrhage he got when he hit a ring post. He had a cut that ran from his eyelid to his skull and required twenty-two stitches.'

Suddenly we see El Apache running towards the aisle closest to our row: he's being chased by two of the *rudos*, or 'tough ones', who corner him against a wall. The woman shouts at the wrestlers again. 'Let him go, fucking rat-tails!' 'I'm a hippie! I'm a hippie!' the guy answers back in a

---

[6] From the popular Mexican children's song 'El Chorrito', by Cri-Cri. 'Allá en la fuente había un chorrito; se hacía grandote, se hacía chiquito.'

mocking tone, puffing out his chest in defiance. Rocío and I focus on the bodies of the wrestlers closest to us: 'You see?' she says after a minute's scrutiny. 'I told you that Fuerza Guerrera was quite a dish. All the others are chubby.' 'Surely they just eat *sopes*',[7] a boy interjects. 'And what about the beer?' says another man. I'm surprised how much a wrestler changes when you see him outside the ring. He's just another mortal, and a ridiculously dressed one at that. But what is this transformation that takes place during their performance?

The audience roars passionately. Two rows further down an old lady with a brown skirt and a brown jacket with white dots shakes her jet-black L'Oréal bun topped with a blood-red bow. 'Leave him alone, leave him alone!' Esperanza Rodríguez shouts incessantly. All of a sudden she gets up from her seat and shakes her fist at the ring. She is surprisingly energetic— in contrast to her frail body, her bowed back, and the placid figure of her husband, a man in his sixties with white hair and broad shoulders. I go down to tell her that I've noticed how excited she gets at the wrestling. 'I'm here because of doctor's orders', she says laughing; 'I was very ill, my nerves, and my doctor told me to come here to let off steam. He said, "go somewhere where you can shout; if you can't go to the wrestling, take a cushion in your house and shout very loudly." And now I do this every Sunday.' My friend Carlos Roces also told me about his sister: 'Every time she went to the wrestling her personality changed. She was usually so demure, so traditional, but at a fight she'd start screaming: "Kill him, kill him! Murderer!" Then she'd go back home and was once again an adorable girl who collected *lucha libre* cards.' 'For the fans, Konan is their whole life; that's why I don't get jealous', the hero's girlfriend tells me when we are outside. She's a stunning blonde who drives an immaculate white Mustang. There's a swarm of kids around Konan.

'People need idols', the playwright Víctor Hugo Rascón told me a few days earlier. 'We all need idols', says a man around sixty years old who comes every Sunday to the Revolución Arena with his mother, who must be eighty-five. 'What do you like best about *lucha libre*, madam?' The old lady waves towards the crowd of children following Konan. 'That, that's what I like best', she says as she takes her son by the arm again.

---

[7] A fried tortilla topped with re-fried beans, onion and hot sauce.

VIII. *Stories from Luck Street*

Finally, it is the most natural thing that the inhabitants of Mexico City—who always live for the day and dream of pay day—have enshrined games of chance as part of popular culture. That's why Mexicans take part in the National Lottery, which sets fate in motion and sells little tickets to give everyone the right to dream and leave poverty behind.

There are three spheres on the dais: a huge one on the right-hand side with 50,000 tiny numbered spheres, and two smaller balls with little spheres that show the total amount of each prize. A boy rotates the big sphere, and the other boys spin the two smaller spheres. The first is linked to a tube: the balls roll down it into a glass container. The taller child picks them out with a little stick. On the other side, another boy picks up the balls that show the amount of the prize. They each shout out the numbers. The big moment is when a number matches a big prize. In the middle of the dais, an older boy repeats the glorious announcement: 'Number 4,572, number 4,572: 80 million pesos! Eeeeeeeighty million!' The ceremony lasts for an hour. A brief moment, charged with meaning, an immense wheel of fortune. Fifty thousand chances to alter your fortune. All eyes focus on the dais of the Lottery Hall, and for sixty minutes—a ritual time?—everybody becomes a traveller. Because travelling is a quest for something and every quest is an expedition. But what is this special traveller, moving in such an intimate space, looking for? Chava Flores asks what Mexicans look for in their dreams.[8] Because to dream is to travel, and travelling opens up a parenthesis in daily time, allowing us access to another time, in this case the promise of a different future that takes shape in a blink of an eye in the dreamer's mind. The promise of Health, Money and Love. The lottery is a key that leads, if chance so decrees, to financial prosperity, a way of breaking free from the biblical punishments on earth. 'You will earn your bread by the sweat of your brow.' But it can also be a way of going towards something, of finding a place for desire. Or a habit that gives rhythm to the passing of the days. Or an occupation that gives life a visible meaning, a structure. For instance, the life of the woman who started 'selling luck' (*vendiendo la suerte*) when she became a widow and had to support her eleven children. Or it is perhaps the extreme symbol of resignation: 'The day I cannot buy a lottery ticket or a cigar, that's when things will be really bad.' Or the other way round, a way of preventing hope from dying: 'Imagine: for an old man who lives only from his IMSS pension, the ticket

---

[8] Chava Flores is a Mexican singer and composer.